SMALL TOWN
PSY-FEMME-VAMPIRE CULTS
AND THE QUIET MAN

ZANE NEWITT

First published 2021
by Rowanvale Books Ltd
The Gate
Keppoch Street
Roath
Cardiff
CF24 3JW
www.rowanvalebooks.com

A CIP catalogue record for this book is available from the British Library.
Paperback ISBN: 978-1-913662-14-1
Hardback ISBN: 978-1-913662-16-5
eBook ISBN: 978-1-913662-15-8

CONTENTS

CHAPTER 1
DO NOT READ THIS BOOK
LOUD DISCLOSURES AND THE
HYPOCRISY OF EMOTION

Herein is a sea of contradiction awash in maddening hypocrisy begotten by emotionalism, romanticism and pain.

On the one hand it stresses free will and personal accountability, making declaratory shouts of 'no types!', eschewing fatalism and positing that choice drives all things. On the other it sets forth profiles, algorithms and formulas to spot covert female narcissists from a mile away.

(What kind of vehicles do they drive? From what sorts of towns and demographics do they hail? How do they dress? What are their feigned interests? What sort of jobs do they hold? And moreover, why are they targeting YOU?)

What follows is sharply anti-psychiatry, anti-academia and unashamedly anti-convention. Why then does it parasitically borrow psychiatric terms, use academic notions and findings, and rest upon conclusions of the same conventions it denounces?

The piece dismisses the notion that narcissists exist at all, or at most that they are reserved for the fraction of a fraction of serial killers that roam the countryside seeking to kill, steal and destroy lives. Then it reverses course to opine in great detail that there *are* female narcissists, very much within the mainstream, and their main *Modus Operandi* is to study material about narcissism, weaponize it, and use it to destroy men.

The volume is an unrelenting alligator's death-roll, thrashing and gnashing at the behavior of these women – then, with equal and measured devotion to the extreme, it seeks to forgive them, for none of us are good; all should be understood and receive empathy, forgiveness and love.

A writer writes. And what should a writer write? He or she should write what they know, what they live, of the small postage-stamp-sized square of the great cosmic elephant they see every day.

I am not a professional psychologist, psychiatrist or relationship expert, and make no claims to the same. I am a father, folklorist, historian, poet, consultant, business owner, and sometimes bro-ken-hearted romanticist. Let the reader decide what yields more applicable advice; their journals or my deductions, their philosophy or my experientialism.

This book is for men, but women will greatly benefit from its perspectives.

For young men, avoid everything in this dark discourse by heeding me: **STAY MARRIED!**

The most honorable man I've ever known happens to be my former father-in-law. Hung aeons ago, in his family's kitchen there is a faded, yellow, cross-stitched, framed saying, likely sewn when cross-stitching was a cool end-of-evening hobby ere bedtime (a time before iPhones and digital sleep-aids), which reads: *"Choose Thy Love, Love Thy Choice".*

Outside of the Bible itself, can words truer be found? Naye!

Let the Great Conversation carry on the grand (albeit circular and unknowable) debate about whether we can control 'falling in love'; whether it be cosmic or chemical, happenstance or fate, is not within the scope of these pages – but I emphatically assert that the 'after falling' doth become a choice.

For "love loves."

We choose to say good morning.

We choose to open doors, to wait to eat, to honor with our whole being.

We choose to learn what kind of coffee or tea she likes.

We choose to find nuanced, fun and kind ways to serve her.

We choose to write pithy notes by hand, hiding them that she might haply find them in the sock drawer or her gym bag.

We choose to find occupation and work our arses off for her.

We choose to be responsive, active listeners.

We choose to court and to flirt, not for six months, but forever.

We choose to apologize when wrong.

We choose to love intentionally, and to love hard.

The sum of our daily micro-choices determines if we are blessed enough to stay married.

For make no mistake, young reader, there are a surplus of good women and very few worthy men. Therefore, make the choices that you lose her not – for you, and not she, will be the worse for it.

Let young lovers read, gleaning from horror stories *of 'what not to become'*.

When marriage occurs in the flower of youth:

- She is not made to bear the baggage of another passenger, and neither are you.
- The culture of "self" and extreme introspection cannot poison you, for you develop your idiosyncrasies, annoying habits, and worldview together, being oil and oil from the beginning (in the stead of oil and water).
- The spiritual consequences of many lovers cannot crowd your union.
- The hurt of 'comparative statements' or 'hinting' is not possible.
- Your financial struggles of youth, student debt and lower-paying, entry-level jobs forges a grit and teamwork that results in strength and commitment not found with two "independent professionals coming together".
- You learn how to fight fair.

- Your opportunity at legacy and what you pass onto your children is infinitely more glorious and healthy for the generation that you bring forth.

Conflict? Choose to stay married.

Season of diminishing flame? Choose to stay married.

Job loss and economic woes? Choose to stay married.

Communication walls? Choose to stay married.

Illness or injury? Choose to stay married.

Did she hurt you? Choose to stay married.

Did she betray you? Choose to love her enough to stay married.

If it be possible, in ANY circumstance, YOU CHOOSE TO STAY MARRIED.

And Thou, Young Man, own these things; suffer wrong, be gentle, be kind, lead but do not overbear, forgive quickly; let not the sun set on your anger, and consider in every action the ends thereof. The long game is for true lovers; 'tis a marathon and no sprint.

Is what I am doing right now going to negatively impact the dream of us passing into death on a park bench, holding hands and laughing when eighty-nine?

If yes, stop it. Stay married.

Did she hurt you? Stay married.

Did she betray you? Choose to love her enough to stay married.

If it be possible, in ANY circumstance, YOU CHOOSE TO STAY MARRIED.

And so, for young, happy men, this book is not for you.

But! For those of us who have stumbled in this regard, there is grace, there is hope: faint not! Although, as the Apostle Paul teaches in Scripture, "You will have troubles in the flesh"[1] (all of your days), you *can* find love again, you can forgive your wrongs, and where wronged, start anew. It is possible and it happens every day.

There are 7.5 billion of us sojourning through this difficult, dark and beautiful life. There is another someone for you.

---

1   1 Corinthians 7:28

But alas, there are also pitfalls, dangers and, yes, monsters roaming the countryside. (And by countryside, I mean countryside – more on that later). Where men looking for love after thirty are concerned, we find two species that would rob you of all joy, crushing all that you are:

The Vampire
The Werewolf

Modernity would call these the Covert Narcissist and the Extroverted or Outward Narcissist.

The Vampire, or more accurately, the Psychic-Vampire (or *Psy-Vamp*) is the scope, yet not the subject, of this book. YOU, o broken-hearted like-gendered friend, are the subject. This is not a revenge book, nor an occasion at lashing out or crying, "Woe is me!" You own your responses in this life, and every choice and action is upon your shoulders only. Those obsessed with the field of this particular genre of 'Self-Help' seek a victim round every corner, a demon under every stone. Their response is bitter, robotic and ever the same, namely:

Leave your partner. Hurt them predictively before they can hurt you (again). No contact. *Discard and devalue.*

Such guidance furthers our divorce culture, licenses many to become the very monsters they oppose, and creates a steady supply of victims and patients all too willing but hopelessly duped into dolling out $150 per hourly session to the 'Victim-Makers', the Nobility of all Narcissists themselves – counselors, psychiatrists and therapists.

They cannot help you.

They are tenfold sicker than you.

They get off on hearing your stories. They live your pains, hurts and secrets by proxy.

By contrast, this book does not support reactive break-ups, unrealistic 'walking away' or cold, logical statements of what you 'ought to do'.

Indeed, the manner in which it may provide aid, if at all, depends entirely upon the stage of love's embrace in which the poor fellow finds himself.

If you happen upon this book and you are in brand new, intense love where she is your first and last thought already, hardly will the markers, traits and characteristics break the spell. Indeed they cannot, for "love loves". You cannot undo this. For you, the volume will do nothing now. But when the cheating, lying and fanged syphoning of your life essence begins, or when she discards you, it will be a help and comfort, peradventure to understand the 'why?', in some measure compressing the healing season that you might rise again.

If you read this book and the development of your relationship is more measured, slower, less intense (but by no means less valuable or important), then red flags, loud behavioral markers and warnings may help you to further scrutinize and slow your approach – or, indeed, terminate the relationship ere the intense flavor of love blossoms and it is too late for you.

If single and looking, do not change your verve and wanton openness for life! If you find yourself liking a Vampire, what can you do save love her? But, let this reading add caution and hesitation, helping you on your quest.

And if a female reader?

There are millions of publications, essays, treatises and tomes regarding male narcissism. And why should there not be? Most men are jerks; most abusers are men; well-rounded, self-actualized knights who provide, defend and, at the same time, cultivate and encourage the "feminine divine" are scant.

For that small remnant, guidance, knowledge-sharing, support, perspectives, and the open sharing of experiences, shortcomings, failings, triumphs and other resources are extremely limited in the Market of Ideas. Therefore, this volume contributes a small part to balancing the gender perspective; and there is tremendous value for women in seeking to understand how we think, how we process, feel and respond.

No punches are pulled, neither quarter given. In these pages men are called to be accountable, to put their wives and significant others first, to exercise empathy, to serve, and to equitably invest into the 'love-bank' with all their might. Through those strong encouragements and comparisons of what not to do, there is value in women getting some glimpse into the male roadmap and playbook.

Alas, thirty-and-above male recovering from a bad, broken relationship, *you* are indeed the subject – you *can* be a Modern-Day Knight in a post-modern, post-truth world; may this book help you as it may! But the Psy-Vamp is the scope.

I have not known romantically the Werewolf, and can only document her motives and approach academically. As we write what we know, and I've known a *small coven* of Vampires, let me help you learn of them and their ways.

The objective of both the Vampire and Werewolf is in every part identical, only differing in means, methods and flavor:

The female narcissist would turn you into the Quiet Man and, once turned, leave you (else cause you to suffer a life abiding her infidelity, if she chooses to keep you in her collection) for being the Quiet Man she turned you into.

CHAPTER 2
UNPOPULAR, REVOLUTIONARY TRUTHS AND MAXIMS

Prior to putting forth a survival guide for the broken and the bruised – varnish for the tarnished knights of the modern realm – some revolutionary and unpopular truths need to be stated.

Of course they are only revolutionary in the sense that they used to be non-sequitur, common-sense matters of fact to every adult toiling through life in Western Civilization. But these truths have been obfuscated and, in many regards, eliminated outright; and society is the worse for it. Thus, as we are now blind to the self-evident, I declare:

Unpopular Revolutionary Truth #1 – Man is not essentially Good. He is essentially Fallen, and at the same time has Free Will and personal responsibility for his choices and actions.

The whole of Modernism, Post-Modernism, Post-Truth-ism, along with the sum of all 'isms' borne of Humanism (and the abandonment of reason), when deconstructed, declares:

Man is essentially good. X is the primal problem; he is the product of X; he is fated by X; thus he is not accountable for his actions.

X is undeviatingly his penis, his father, his mother, his socio-economic circumstance, his environment, his chemical composition, his genetics, and/or the pigmentation particles in his skin.

This fatalistic view demands an external force, an engineer or an Elite to 'fix' what ails Man. But, as it does so, the view plunges silently into its own abyss void of logic, the choke of the serpent eating its own tail in a circular and self-annihilating field of weeds. For are not the Elite comprised of Men? Who, then, fixes them?

Often this objection is answered by the fact that nearly every therapist in turn sees their own therapist, and that therapist likewise his or her own therapist, *ad infinitum*. This of course renders useless the need for any therapist at all, as the premise of fatalism is that one is fated, and if fated one cannot be fixed. And if the Elite are also of Man, then the Elite cannot fix Man, for the Elite are also fated to be the product of their penises, parents, genes and traumas.

And so the whole of Modern Humanism is well captured in the parable of the Blind Mice or the Scriptural adage of the Blind Guides.

Teenagers who don't quite 'fit' the expectations of their State School Collectives see through the nonsense of this all; they are the ones with tattoos and piercings that tell the counselors to "fuck off" and to "deal with their own shit" instead of imposing their nonsensical pop psychology on the kid who just wants to love, be loved, and be left alone.

But what the sixteen-year-old sees the masses do not; and the churn of industry to perpetuate a Nation of Victims cycles on.

Germane to this prose, with deep recognition that *ideas have consequences,* is that *they* assert that the Narcissist:

- Is fated to be a narcissist through X (insert any of the above as desired)
- Is fated to be a narcissist due to self-esteem imbalances
- Cannot change

Were it any other diagnosed or presupposed 'disorder', the next bullet would read:

- Is not accountable for his or her actions and must be treated through therapy

But with the Narcissist, rather the *Male Narcissist*, the careful observer will note a subtle change in the rule illuminating hints and markers of Feminism bearing upon and indeed reshaping Psychology:

- IS accountable for his actions, must be punished for his actions, cannot be treated with therapy

The capstone of this premise, when considering the worldview that states *All are Products of X and Fated to Y*, is a first and early clue that some force, group or spirit is seeking to create a Boogie Man. And do not folklore and the casual observation of history tell us that tyrants and monsters clothe themselves as heroes by creating a monster to slay?

The truth is that:

Man is essentially flawed or fallen; nothing makes him do anything; he is accountable for his own actions, which are the product of Free Will.

Flawed but accountable? Paradoxical? Certainly. True? Emphatically!

Like Humanism, the Judeo-Christian worldview acknowledges that there is a problem. There is brokenness, there is despair, there are relationship struggles, injustices a-plenty, and death. But agreement diverges with regards to both the origin and solution for the problem – a gulch between incompatible worldviews that cannot be breached.

- When you chose to be cruel instead of kind, your penis did not make you do it.
- When you chose to be jealous instead of happy for the success of your classmate, your daddy didn't make you do it.
- When you chose to shoplift from the convenience store, your circumstances didn't make you do it.
- When you chose to violate the rights and property of others, the pigmentation in your skin particles is not to blame.

Like the Humanists, I concur that an outside force must be accessed to fix the problem. Diverging from the Humanist, I reject fatalism and assert free agency.

We groan and agonize in our flesh knowing that we will err, we will mess up, we will fall short – but I, and I alone, am the problem. And because I am the problem, only I can be the solution to the problem. But because I am the problem, I can't possibly be the solution. Thus we turn to God, to grace, and to His love to empower us to "get back up and do better and try not to do it again."

The simple truths that:

- We are flawed
- There is a God
- I am not Him
- I will make mistakes
- I own my mistakes
- He loves me
- I need to get back up!

constitute the end of the entire enterprise working to perpetuate the Nation of Victims. Apropos to a treatise touching on so-called Narcissists is the extreme minority view that:

- They choose their actions
- Thus they can choose to change their actions

And that certainly includes the Psychic Vampire Femme Narcs roaming about consuming, draining and destroying men. You, ladies, are choosing to reduce strong males into The Quiet Man. You are willing monsters and, far from declaring a death sentence or droning on and on about how you cannot change or how you should be banished, dismissed and punished, I rather declare that you *can change*. God has judged ALL guilty that He might have mercy upon All. You can fight the factors and drivers in your vain imagination and choose, by your free will, to support, encourage and cultivate healthy masculinity in your partners, in the same way your partners ought to do all to serve the splendor and complexity of the feminine within you!

The next earth-shattering declaration – one sure to see this book burned and advocative commentary shut down on every social media platform – is:

Unpopular Truth #2 – There are very, very few, if any, actual individuals with Narcissistic Personality Disorder. Or really, with any "disorder" (see Unpopular Truth #1). It's a scam, a ploy, a trend and a fad to fabricate Boogie Men for the Nation of Victims and to give license to any one person to horribly abuse any other person, provided they first label the object of their abuse a Narcissist.

According to mainstream academia, the hallmarks of narcissistic personality disorder (NPD) are extreme grandiosity, a total lack of empathy, and an overwhelming, all-consuming need for an endless supply of admiration. Others view individuals with this condition as arrogant, self-centered, manipulative, and relentlessly demanding. Typically, they are preoccupied with perpetual elaborate 'hero-fantasies' and are convinced that they deserve special treatment, entitled by invented merit to "sit at the right of God" (or demoting God Himself in preference for themselves).

Per the experts, these characteristics begin in early adulthood and become increasingly evident in multiple contexts, such as at work and in relationships, until the disorder fully establishes itself as the primary and driving personality type.

People with NPD are claimed to often try to associate with other people they believe are unique or gifted in some way, which can enhance their own aggrandizement. They seek excessive admiration and attention and cannot tolerate criticism or defeat.

Indeed, individuals with NPD, according to the *Diagnostic and Statistical Manual of Mental Disorders (DSM)*[2], exhibit five

---

2   Diagnostic and Statistical Manual of Mental Disorders, Fifth Edition, American Psychiatric Association, 2013

or more of the following, which are present by early adulthood and across contexts:

- A grandiose sense of self-importance
- Preoccupation with fantasies of unlimited success, power, brilliance, beauty, or ideal love
- Belief that one is special and can only be understood by or associate with special people or institutions
- A need for excessive admiration
- A sense of entitlement (to special treatment)
- Exploitation of others
- A lack of empathy
- Envy of others or the belief that one is the object of envy
- Arrogant, haughty behavior or attitudes

Individuals with NPD cannot abide criticism or defeat, and may react with disdain or anger – but social withdrawal or the false appearance of humility may also follow, according to the *DSM*.[3]

Researchers have reported associations between NPD and high rates of substance abuse and mood or anxiety disorders. These may be attributable to characteristics such as impulsivity and the increased experience of shame in people with NPD.

With typical vagueness, the experts conclude that the causes of narcissistic personality disorder are not yet well-understood. Genetic and biological factors, as well as environment and early life experiences, are all thought to play a role in the development of this condition.

Lastly, it is stated that NPD cannot be cured. Treatment for narcissistic personality disorder can be challenging, since people with this condition present with a great deal of grandiosity and defensiveness, making it difficult for them to acknowledge problems and vulnerabilities. It is possible that psychotherapy may be useful in helping people with narcissistic personality disorder relate to others in a healthier and more compassionate way.[4]

---

3   Narcissistic Personality Disorder, psychologytoday.com
4   Narcissistic Personality Disorder, psychologytoday.com

Suffice it to say that this definition can be, and is, the most weaponized and misused set of criteria for any person going through a break-up in the twenty-first century. If you've done this to an ex, stop it. If you've done it chronically, on purpose and with ill intent, then you might be a Psychic Vampire. *Please stop it.*

Attribute	What she says during the courtship and early stages of the relationship	What she says after the break-up
High achiever in business	Ambitious, special! Go-getter! Provider!	Narcissist
Wants to provide better future for his children than he had growing up	Ambitious, special! Go-getter! Provider!	Narcissist
Competitiveness	Wants to be the best! Such a hard worker!	Narcissist
Tries to distinguish himself romantically and not be like all the other guys	He's so 5D! He's in tune with emotions and what women want!	Narcissist
Has strong boundaries about how he is treated	Treats me well and expects to be treated equally as well. Admirable and strong!	Narcissist

And on and on it goes. Any attribute of strength, conviction, ambition or striving for excellence can be converted and contorted into narcissism.

The actual narcissist possesses the deification of his or her own will and has complete understanding of a code; a program that they run to intentionally hurt and destroy others. Simply being a jerk or having a bad day does not a narcissist make.

Because men are bombarded with accusations of being narcs on a daily basis, some might even, through the course of time and volume, begin to believe it. Below is a better test to help a person determine if they have NSD.

Do you have the self-actualization to consider whether you are or are not a narcissist? Yes? Then you're not one.

Do own your mistakes? Yes? Then you're not a narcissist.

Do you possess the ability to consider the feelings, views and rationale of others? Yes? Again, not a narcissist.

Regard and feelings when you see poverty, or the weak and downtrodden suffering? Yes? Not a narcissist.

Kindness for and protection of animals? Yes? Not even close to a narcissist.

Wanting to invent something to improve the world does not make you a narcissist. Wanting to be the best at a sport or an artform does not make you a narcissist. Wanting to maximize how you look for your body type does not make you a narcissist. Wanting to dress nicely and be presentable does not make you a narcissist.

Neither do declarations of how you want to be treated, what kind of love language fills your love-bank, how you like to be communicated with, or expectations of consistent patterns and practices of affection, tradition and romantic rituals make you a narcissist.

Though the popular conclusion is that every man is a narcissist, the truth is that almost no man is.

Unpopular Truth #3 – Unrequited Love, and not Narcissism or "Personality Disorders", lies at the root of most broken relationship scenarios.

The final unpopular, revolutionary truth is another deconstruction, another case of taking what is seemingly complex and boiling it down to that which is very simple. "Love loves, and only equitable love endures."

This is the truth that transcends the others, and is the terminal deathblow for both pop psychology, Modernism, and the "every man is a narcissist" movement.

When a person detects that their partner 'just isn't that into them' and overcompensates with lavish gifts, excess texts or what is mockingly called 'clingy' behavior, the typical analysis is that that person is projecting their insecurity, lack of self-esteem, and abandonment or avoidance issues onto their partner. At its extreme, this leads into controlling behavior that smothers and vacuums the energy out of the hapless victim.

This treatise rejects such thinking and asserts rather that, if you detect that a person isn't that into you then it's because... the person just isn't that into you.

Where couples are jointly and severally investing in the shared 'love-bank', there are no traces of Personality Disorder, Narcissism or even 'Personality Type'. Rather, there are two individuals making daily choices to put their partners first, and to edify them.

If he lies to you, it's because he chose to and doesn't love you enough to be consistently honest. Hard words to receive, but there is no need to search for what 'caused' him to do it; 'twas the absence of equal love.

If he cheats on with you with the Executive Assistant at the office, it's not because of his childhood issues, that his dad cheated on his mom, or because his spouse doesn't please him in the bedroom. He cheated because he chose to cheat, and because he did not love his wife enough to be faithful.

Though a wildly unpopular concept, each of us knows, when facing the mirror, that we ever face the same fork in the road when challenges confront a relationship:

- Choose ourselves
- Choose our partners

Couples that choose their partners during those crucibles remain together, happy and whole for a lifetime. Individuals that choose 'self' die alone with their cats, and their myriad of excuses for what 'made' themselves or their partners do it.

The harshness of this truth is also its grace.

The couples that survive extreme hurts, such as adultery, can and do mend when the offending partner owns this truth: that his or her love wavered and was not equitable for this or that moment, week or season of life, but has returned; and with its return comes accountability and commitment of future, better choices.

When the 'excuse machine' constantly churns there is no hope for a return, no pathway for reconciliation. *There will be always be something* – a factor, trigger or 'reason' for future choices and recycled hurts.

Ironically, the Psychic Vampires decry Narcissism (which can best be described as an unnatural, haughty and extreme love of the Self) as abusive while at the same time deeply disagreeing with this revolutionary truth. To them, it's the Self over the partnership, but their narcissism is simply dressed and masked in self-help, Third-Wave feminist and militant victim vernacular. They excuse their abuses by declaring "Self Above All!", then citing the nine reasons they discarded, lied to, ditched and otherwise sought the destruction of their partners. Much easier to simply own the truth that they don't love these men and move onto the next than to maintain the charade of victimhood.

Why is true love so rare? Why is the divorce rate now above 50%?

Unrequited love.

We find and fall in love with individuals that do not love us back equally. This is the top tragedy of a fallen, sin-cursed world. Because there is no known way to measure whether or not he or she loves you with the same intensity, warmth and undying commitment that you love, the risk of unrequited love is always present.

The couples that seem to be a horrible mismatch on paper but are just as successful and strong as a couple thirty years on simply love each other equally. That's it. That's the secret. The 'perfect couple' that breaks up after three months did not.

Thus, it is a lack of love, not a lack of psychiatric therapy, at the root of brokenness where relationships are concerned.

CHAPTER 3
THEIR OBJECTIVE: THE QUIET MAN

Prior to profiling the Femme Psychic Vampire – making uncomfortable explorations into what makes her tick, how to identify her, and most importantly, what to do to protect yourself as a modern knightly, self-actualized and masculine man – it is vital to start with the end in mind and define her objective.

Therefore I introduce, or rather *reintroduce,* to the reader's recollection (for each of us know and have witnessed many "Quiet Men") the Quiet Man.

Let the reader's own experienced observation and thoughts travel in the mind's eye to that pitiful grandfather, sitting hunkered and bony in his chair (the one thing in the home that is his, the garage or tools and lawnmowers notwithstanding) in the corner of the living room. When not there, he is bidden reluctantly to the table to join the gathering of family and friends for Sunday coffee and crumb-cake.

He is there as a furnishing, not as a valued participant.

His face is sunken.

He is slender, but after the unhealthy manner.

He is pale, regardless of ethnicity or skin tone. He is as a cartoonish apparition of a pirate prisoner sentenced to roam, shackled and shamed, about the hull in a children's adventure movie.

He has Xs where his eyes ought to be, the windows to his soul fogged, cracked... shut.

He is pale, yet he is also green.

And this pale greenness is not a function of chronology but rather a hard, sad life, for you know older gentlemen a decade senior to the Quiet Man. Think now on one of these other fellows; how he is a little plump, cheeks as great, happy, shiny circles of roses, brimming with verve. He is three-score-and-three, yet can talk contemporary film and sports with the teenagers, geopolitics with the college students, religion and worldview with their professors.

His home is his castle, where his spouse is his partner and queen. His table is one of warmth, encouragement and no small measure of fun, pithy banter. He pinches his wife's arse, flirting with her like a sixteen-year-old caught up in new love. Frequently, you spot him holding her hand. He is the life of the party; though his years be golden, he is raging with jolly fight and no fright against the dying of the light. He is the Healthy Man.

Turning back to the Quiet Man: *he* says little, and when he does it proceeds the vigilant, permissive, scowling nod of an Elder Vampire to whom misfortune caused him to be wed. She governs from the Siege Perilous of the family Round Table, dictating the agenda of all discourse (of which ninety-and-four percent constitutes defaming, slandering and 'shit-talking' about neighbors, work colleagues and associates for their myriad pretended crimes, whether the offence occurred yesterday or forty-and-nine years past). He is allowed to grumble an occasional complaint about the weather or speech pertaining to the superficial, provided that such speech does not exceed two or more sentences at any time.

His job is to supply the Vampire – to supply her with his silence. His acquiescence fuels her pride. The absence of his protests, or even his contributions, invigorates her command over the afternoon assembly.

He is not noticed, but she notices that he receives no notice, and it charges her. It feeds her.

The Quiet Man consumes strong drink: bourbon, whiskey, vodka or scotch. He loses himself in the liquid of the sad, the IV of the defeated. The perception is that he is an alcoholic, but he chooses the anesthesia. Tis no addiction, but rather the necessary conduit of escape.

The perception is that he is gruff, an Old Grump, but twenty-thousand-and-nine verbal assaults have conditioned him to choose silence over ridicule, a downward gaze over the scald of boiling boisterousness. A wall of misinterpreted canker to mitigate any further increase to the thousands of punctures, scarred then pecked again and again by the Devil-Hen that possesses his soul.

She would have him *look* masculine before all. As such, he is found in cowboy boots, his fabricated fashion fitted with western shirt, topped with grease-stained and crinkled Stetson. His belt buckle is too large and his jeans too tight. He is permitted to chew (for kissing was forbidden years and years afore) tobacco. The Quiet Man looks as the Marlboro Man, but his chisel is faux; the reality of him is peanut brittle and not cool steel.

Rather than encouraging and cultivating his masculinity, she has suppressed, devalued and robbed him of it. The silent brooding masks an arrested, weakly boy and no man.

He looks strong (in the same manner that an abusive husband has his wife or girlfriend 'dolled up' for appearance's sake), but strength has long since departed the Quiet Man:

- Strength of expression – murdered
- Strength from praise for providing – slain
- Strength from support to create and to compete – killed
- Strength to thrive as a Servant Leader – utterly, triply killed

To lead, to provide, to protect. The three pillars of healthy manhood – so long ago crushed and then swept away that the Quiet Man has forgotten that he has forgotten them. He sits in his chair, staring at the mantel o'er the fireplace. Above the mantel, shelves. One special shelf is high, too high for him to reach. She has the only stepstool in their home and has upon the high shelf placed his testicles in a jar of shame and formaldehyde, his balls frozen in ambience. He stares at them daily, remembering but not remembering what they were for.

He used to feed her appetite via conflict. Drama was her blood, negative adrenaline and trauma her vital essence. But that was transitional. That had an end to it. And the end was submission.

In her active sexual years she cheated on him, countless times. The Quiet Man suspected, but never accused (though she made sport of accusing him of accusing). Had he actually laid the charge, he would have been discarded, and she would have found another boy to morph into her Quiet Man. He suffered it, he enabled it; less so at the first, more so in the end. With each tryst, the jar of shame was placed on a higher shelf, then higher – finally, too, too high.

The Quiet Man is not grumpy. He is cuckolded, he is defeated. Where the infidelity was darkly hidden in never-to-be-discussed shadow, the chronic lying and dishonesty was done, for decades, in the light of day.

The Vampire lies. For lies beget a chain reaction, and in the reaction of drama and trauma she feeds. The self-important need lies, drama and despair in order to feel necessary. The ultimate surrender of not objecting to lies, dropping the countenance and going along with them is the final sign that the Healthy Man is dead and the skeleton of the Quiet Man roams as a zombie in his stead.

The Quiet Man sits at the table as the Vampire spins lies and celebrates tales of slander with her girlfriends, their adult children, their neighbors from church. She lies; his mouth stays shut. She finds occasion to put him down to elevate herself; his mouth stays shut. She sows discord; his mouth stays shut. And she feeds and feeds upon his submission.

"Why not just leave her?" the reasonable cry.

The Quiet Man, before he was such, fell in love with her. From that day to this, he makes a daily choice each morning to love his wife. His love for her stands alone and is not based upon what she does. "Leaving" was never part of his orientation, but he was never given the tools to reclaim his knighthood and his testicles (which probably would have resulted in her leaving him, but also would have spared so many years of systematic death), thus forever to drown without drowning in the tempest of unrequited love.

The Quiet Man loves, but is not loved in return. The Vampire's objective was to create the Quiet Man so she could more freely do that which is in her nature to do.

When you do encounter a man that has finally succumbed to years of being vampiric supply, he is not a drunkard, he is not a grouch. He needs your best, warmest hug, that peradventure a miracle will thaw so iced a heart, scraping away the layers of scars that he might receive love again.

The fullness of the Quiet Man is extreme and less frequent in the current generation, where divorce is more prevalent. More often, men object and fight back at some point on their sad descent from the Healthy Man to the Quiet Man, and a Partial Quiet Man is more common. A spectrum or range exists. But when men object, the favored tool of the Vampire is to transfer the label of "narcissist" from themselves to the Healthy Man.

Castration of the Healthy Man is no easy feat. The Humanists and the Elite require an emasculated, effeminate generation of Men in order to subjugate men, women and children alike. After all, castrated men do not take up arms when the soldiers come knocking at the door; they do not assert their rights when "papers" are demanded. They wear masks when told, walk where told, march as told.

The heart of real masculinity is a love of liberty, a love of protecting children and supporting the feminine divinity of their mates, sisters and friends. Modernity would destroy these virtues, and the Quiet Man ensures removal of the only physical line of defense against the same.

To this end, the Modernists and the Elites needed only spark a wave of feminism and ignite anger and evangelical fervor amongst a very small percentage of the female population. The Modernists and the Elites did not create the Vampires (for, as covered earlier, each individual has Free Will, and personal accountability); rather, their fiery rage lit the caverns that flushed them out; then they formalized a playbook for them to follow. This resulted in methodology, pattern, protocol and practice for uniting Femme Vampires into Covens... and multiplying the production of Quiet Men.

CHAPTER 1
WHENCE COMETH THE FEMME VAMPIRE?
SMALL-TOWN BITTERNESS
AND THE HUBRIS OF ESCAPISM

In popular culture, literature and film, a psychic vampire differs from the sanguine or 'blood vampire' in that it feeds upon energy instead of blood. For the typical Nosferatu, life is in the blood – but for this special breed sustenance hangs upon a recurring supply of drama, emasculating defeat of prey, exhaustive energy, emotional eggshells, devaluation, and spiritual and mental destruction.

Femme Psychic Vampires are not just 'rude' or *bitches,* as the pejorative goes; they are women who have learned (typically via mentorship but sometimes through study) and implemented a coalesced actual handbook complete with methods, principles and tactics to devour once-living men, leaving only the Quiet Man behind as a carcass. These methods, principles and tactics will be covered after we introduce *The Vampire Profile.*

Theirs is a willful and designed intention: an aim to do their part in serving the societal reshaping goals of the Counter-Culture Elite at the macro, and to achieve empowerment and a deeply perverse sense of independence at the micro or individual level.

Small, rural areas tend to be the optimal breeding grounds where the forces of evil find and develop new vampires for their worldwide coven.

A suggested précis and sample journey into darkness for the Small-Town Psychic Vampire follows.

First, and foundationally, she is beautiful. Stunningly so. From her middle-school years (or earlier) she is self-aware (and moreover, constantly *made aware)* that her looks far exceed those of her peers; in school, in town, in the county. Though there are a hundred of her equals in New York or Scottsdale, she and one or two others share the spotlight in her environment.

One or two others...

This is critical, as she does have rivals, or perceived competition. The others don't view her as a rival, because they don't operate from a 'compare and contrast' worldview. These choose a far different path: they are the *Small-Town Fully Actualized Goddesses*, the heroines of our heartland, the treasures of their counties and the country that each of us know.

They are:

- Kind
- Confident but humble
- Devoid of pretense
- Strong and temperate
- Fun and outgoing
- Endowed with seemingly divine intuition and wisdom
- Empathetic

They:

- Love children, love animals
- Have a circle of friends of every shape, creed, color, and economic and social standing/popularity level
- Are equally content to go on to great things in a large city or stay in their/a similar small town to pursue career, marriage and happiness
- Are driven to compete in the market of ideas, not for attention or status
- Are not governed by their upbringing
- Are focused on where they are going, not whence they came.

The Psychic Vampire is an introvert. Or, more accurately, she feigns the persona of an introvert (and as she ages and reads articles and personality tests, intentionally emulates the attributes suggested as attributable to the same.) The Psy Vamp loathes the Small-Town Fully Actualized Goddesses (for, in the final analysis, feminism *is* the hatred of women) almost as much as she loathes men, her *covert* abhorrence towards them a fundamental part of her constitution.

The mainstream refers to the male variety as 'Covert Narcissists', and like them the Psychic Vampire is covert; quiet and sullen and brooding in most of her operations.

Like the designation and transference of the wildly overused 'narcissist' for her targets, the introvert label is her *carte blanche* for the sum of her Crazy Making Behavior. Introversion ranks amongst the most weaponized pop-psychology fads of our era. The obsession of identification with a Personality Type of any sort – to the exclusion of individual responsibility and Free Will – is what empowers the Femme Narcissist to chronically and with lunacy and audacity justify the draining abuses of her mates, children, family and co-workers. *"I'm not being mean, I'm just an introvert"* goes the mantra.

Sample Behavior or Situation	What the Psy Femme Vamp Says	What the Rest of Us Know	What the Truth is
Coldly glaring at spouse with far-off, murderous stare	"I'm an introvert!"	In a relationship you have a responsibility to be nice to your partner and choose not to glare at them.	The Psy Vamp is coldly glaring at you so that you will react. She hopes that you will either 1) react or 2) start/continue your journey to being the Quiet Man. If you react, she will deflect from her actions and make it about your response, then feed on the drama and trauma.
Doesn't greet you in the bookstore, randomly acts like you don't exist	"I'm an introvert!"	In a relationship you have a responsibility to be nice to your partner and choose to treat them the same way regardless of environment or circumstance.	The Psy Vamp is suddenly acting like you don't exist at the bookstore so that you either 1) react or 2) start/continue your journey to being the Quiet Man. If you react, she will deflect from her actions and make it about your response, then feed on the drama and trauma.

At the pub, suddenly loses herself in her mobile device mid-conversation, chewing her gum like she is mad at it. The nice bartender asks her many engaging questions in order to bring her back into the conversation. She ignores him, creating deep awkwardness for you.	"I'm an introvert!"	In a relationship you have a responsibility to read the ebb and flow of a conversation in a public setting and provide positive contributions where possible	The Psy Vamp has suddenly lost herself in her mobile device and made angry masticating love to her chewing gum to be covertly dismissive to you in public. She hopes that you will either 1) react or 2) start/continue your journey to being the Quiet Man. If you react, she will deflect from her actions and make it about your response, then feed on the drama and trauma.
You had a whimsical, romantic time shopping and just scored her a new pair of designer shoes. She appears to be having a great time until the cashier, a female, starts joining in your playful and excited banter. She will not look the cashier	"I'm an introvert!"	In a relationship you will have public encounters with the opposite gender. You have a responsibility to your partner to keep the situation fun, neighborly and light to the edification of all three participants	The Psy Vamp cheats on you chronically (whether text-cheating, emotional cheating, 'just-a-friend' cheating, or actual cheating that involves sexual congress.) She does not feel guilt for this, but she does desire to overcompensate for her infidelity with extreme pretense of perverted concepts of loyalty through the display of angered quiet to other women – especially at

in the eye and awkwardly ceases talking, leaving you to carry the now cooling conversation with the cashier. The great fun connected to the shoes has turned to fear over what you did wrong			the store, in church, or at the pub. Additionally, the over-compensation manifests as the constant signalling of obsessive possession. A constant "He is my victim/prey, get out!" Her desire is to create a reaction so that she can transfer her cheating to you and rage against you over pretended infidelities for simply being kind to other women at the store. She hopes that you will either 1) react or 2) start/continue your journey to being the Quiet Man. If you react, she will deflect from her actions and make it about your response, then feed on the drama and trauma

The Psychic Vampire chooses to develop her persona schema at a young age through the conduit of a ruminating, cold introversion (the opposite to how the Werewolf creates and devours the Quiet Man, which must be the scope of another treatise by those more familiar with that monster) and via the primary drive of contempt – contempt for her small town; bitterness and rancor of feeling entitled for *more*.

The trailer park; the handsy uncle; the stench of the farm; the monotony of the same two low-class department stores and one fuel station; the gossip; the intrusion. The poorly groomed boys sharing her and boasting of it; moreover, those whose boasts were false, but her reputation allowed for no recompense for their lies.

The constant internal kneading and gnawing that something is wrong with this place, coupled with the ongoing delusional development and crystallization that nothing is wrong with *her*. The teachers; the pastors; the rumors. The constant rasp, as if from a devil vulture ever perched upon a branch protruding from her shoulder, cawing at all times, "Get out, go far, go far from here, get out, get out!"

And from delusion is born arrogance; a haughty spirit and disdain for anything and everyone associated with her town, her county, and *all* small towns. In her nuclear DNA, the Psy Vamp believes herself to be better than the town, better than the townsmen, and certainly better than her family, who had the outrageous audacity to birth such a shiny gem in the coalmines of rural America instead of Beverly Hills or New York City.

She is beautiful.

She is a self-diagnosed introvert.

Third and lastly, the Small-Town Psychic Vampire perceives herself as poor.

Though her parents likely own property or even manage a small business, the Vampire believes it is *not enough* to sponsor her escape (elsewise they wouldn't have lived in that Podunk Villa in the first place). Later in life, once she has escaped her falsely perceived prison, she will appropriate an anti-materialistic veneer, presenting herself as a 'hippie' or an 'enlightened wealthy woman that does not need things', but in the formative years hers is a drive to escape.

Lacking finance for this, she looks to the social program that will best afford her travel, title and assumed respect; the Psychic Vampire often joins the military, or is heavily associated with the Armed Forces. For what could be better than a lifelong paycheck (feeding her extreme sense of entitlement) and the pseudo-humble, brooding 'look at me, but don't look at me, I'm important' that the military affords?

She will be beautiful.

She will be a self-diagnosed introvert.

She will find an escape, often via the military or public life, that 'gets her out'.

She will have an utter and insatiable hatred for her town, and her family.

And once freed from the prison of her confines... she will feed.

CHAPTER I
WOMEN IN BLAZERS HARBORING HATRED OF HOMEMAKERS, CHOICE AND OTHER WOMEN

Although Free Will, personal responsibility and the molding of one's character, social energy and personality is ultimately a choice, and although the Vampire begins to become the creature that will one day vacuum the souls from future men during her time *in the small town*, I postulate that the Femme Vampire experiences her full metamorphosis from mortal to monster through the channel of two cataclysmic events:

- The Psychic Vampire truly falls in love once – usually early in life – but it is unrequited.
- The Psychic Vampire is discovered by/otherwise finds a like-minded mentor (or coven, but always with a leader). There is a terminal event where she stands at the fork in the road and is externally 'nudged' down the path of covert narcissism.

Unrequited Love

We live in a cruel, cursed and fallen world. Nowhere does this manifest more profoundly than when:

Person A loves Person B at 100%, and Person B loves Person A at 10%.

This tragic truth is no respecter of gender, background, age group, culture or creed. It creates an unrelenting hurt. The subject of plays, sonnets, movies and a myriad of songs, paintings and sculptures, no pain is more expressed, or more explored, than the pangs of despised, one-way love.

When the starry-eyed and unfortunate lass or fellow is oblivious of their unequal investment and find out dramatically (perhaps they are randomly 'ghosted', or receive a Dear John letter) the impact is tantamount to the sudden loss of a family member to a tragic accident. It is truly *as death*.

No closure.

No preparation.

No goodbye.

The trauma may take months, years or forever to heal, and the temptation is great for the individual to:

- Never trust again
- Never invest fully again
- Become extremely guarded
- Become as a hermit or recluse
- Shut down where love and romance are concerned

Each of these and more are a natural, normal desire emanating from a broken heart; those who have suffered such deserve empathy, warmth, a listening ear, grace, patience and time to heal and express their healing as they see fit.

Alternatively, a partner may realize very early on that their love is unrequited. As *Love loves* and *Love stands on its own merits*, they may remain in the relationship and exercise their active love, hoping their partner one day changes and does the same. This is the 'slow death', and can result in:

- Desperate clinginess
- Over-effort
- Slow and then metastatic growth of distrust and jealousy issues
- Strife
- Ongoing loss of motivation

- Codependence
- Loss of self-worth

The negative stimulus is supernaturally weighty, the yoke grave for those coming through the other side of one of these slow-death relationships, and they likewise have a tendency to:
- Ask too many validation questions early in a relationship
- Constantly evaluate the investments by their partner
- Press for determination and the classification of a new relationship prematurely
- Become overbearing
- Go through many mini 'start-stop' relationships as a result of the primal unrequited love incident

Each of these likewise are natural, normal results of a broken heart; I reiterate, those who have suffered such deserve empathy, warmth, a listening ear, grace, patience and time to heal and express their healing as they see fit.

The Psychic Vampire experiences unrequited love and, rather than healing in a natural way, or even lashing out in a season or two of vitriol, chooses to conceal the reality of this trauma, and instead visits the very thing that hurt her onto future partners. The extreme claims of introversion become a cover story for the wounded to brood, and to hunt for someone to pay.

Thus men must note that the woman lying to them, emasculating them, baiting-and-switching or otherwise draining their essence is not an overly complex villain. Rather, she is *the small-town girl who lost in love with the soldier boy that left her*, and she's taking it out on you and anything else with a penis.

Because the Vampire must assert that all men are narcissists and worthy only of being devalued or re-programmed into the Quiet Man, she will never, under any circumstance, confess that she simply loved deeply and lost. Especially after she brands *the Ex* as a narcissist in her efforts to edify (falsely) her new prey (*"You are nothing like him, thank God!"*) during the love-bombing build-up.

Having escaped her small town – the silt and soot of its short-comings and lesser bumpkins; having found career and admiration in the public life only to find someone (often a soldier, an officer) and be burned, the Psychic Vampire kindles an actual hatred for men, a wrath of biblical proportions. Moreover does her wrath engender venomous envy for women in traditional roles who enjoy the fruits of healthy relationships, contentment and happiness.

"How could he not love ME!" she cries.

And indeed, most all adults have been in her straits. Where we healed (or didn't heal, but chose to not visit vengeance on our neighbors for it), she hated. Where we moved on, she morphed. Morphed into a stealthy man-killing assassin.

She runs in conservative circles, but she is the antithesis of conservative. She abhors mothers above all others, for she is no longer capable of, neither can abide, being around those giving daily and unyielding, selfless love with the expectation of nothing in return. The Psychic Vampire is foretold in Scripture: is she not the person *without natural affection* referenced in the Apostle Paul's second letter to Timothy?[5]

The Vampire already invested love once, and the soldier or pilot recompensed nothing but grief to her in return. She will sooner be damned than suffer that kind of arrangement again; not even to a child. Not even with *her child.* For this cause most Psychic Vampires are childless. If they do procreate, it is quite 'by accident' and the child becomes an object useful for making the Vampire look wonderful before all – the yelling, neglect and devaluation that occurs behind the scenes notwithstanding.

But in conservative circles she runs, nonetheless.

Conservative men have strength. And she must syphon, consume and, where there are leftovers, banish to the outer void all masculine energy. She feeds it as a one-way pipeline into the hole within her soul. A hole for which there is no propitiation. A hole excavated

---

5   2 Timothy 3:3

in the small town, quarried by unrequited love, and breached full through to the abyss by choice and intention.

As for weakness... Paradoxically, she abhors weak men, except that they start off strong and are *made weak* by her processes. The Vampire does not like to make company with the handiwork of others any more than the fox has no preference for the company of the dead chickens one farm over.

To draw near unto her profiled chickens, she must look the part of one she *perceives* as desirable by conservative men (remember, individuals 'like who they like, and typology equals mythology'): conservative; domestic; unassuming; mousey; kind.

And the women. How she hates the women! For these fellow possessors of vaginas have bought into a worldview and structure whereby they actually:

- Recognize that men and women are different
- Support the function of men as provider and protector in the home
- Encourage masculinity

These are cardinal, unforgivable sins worthy of contempt, endless privy slander and smack talk, strife and unsustainable drama. As the Vampire cries about introversion, in reality she destroys and then withdraws from peer groups because she hates women who do not hate men.

But circumstance and occasion cause her sometimes to be amongst the women. When she is around them in a social setting, her contempt for them causes her physical illness, her quiet contempt barely hidden by pressed lips and forced smiles. She suffers as she suffers them, until one day by chance she is marked by one of her own... and then everything changes.

The Mentor

It is important to restate and affirm that most monsters roaming the countryside are in fact men.

Men tend towards unhealthy, controlling attributes.

Men tend towards laziness and a lack of purposeful thoughtfulness.

Men commit physical abuse more, both as a count and percentage, than women.

Men are prone to hollering, degrading and belittling.

Men play games with money and other currencies of leverage.

However, what Wolfmen and Male Vampires are in quantity, their female counterparts make up for in *quality*. For though they be few, Hell hath no fury as a well-seasoned, trained and focused female narcissist.

These Adepts have honed their skills, stacking scores of skulls in a sepulcher of Self over many decades. These have fed, and fed, and drained the land dry of testosterone. Ironically, having no more men to eat, these narcissists do something that is quite contrary to narcissism (if only the subject matter were not sinister): they seek to pass on their skills and actually teach other women to be as they.

Perhaps this too is self-centered, in the sense that they (as with each of us) seek to continue 'themselves' through reproduction. But on some level, they have a true fondness; a fellowship amongst manhaters.

The Mentor, the Queen Mother Vampire, has read every article, has perverted every school of behavioral academics, has mastered the power of linguistics, has perfected victimization, has enjoyed a lengthy run as a professional abuser and manslayer. When she stumbles upon (nay, targets) the *Small-Town Woman Struggling with Unrequited Love* who shows flashes of wit, exudes anger, can command the room through inversion (the art of brooding and drawing attention via pretending to eschew attention) and is predisposed to a mighty selfish streak, the Mentor, perhaps long dormant, grows her fangs, piercing the neck of the Small-Town Woman, imbuing her with potent poison, injecting her with generations of lore and doctrine (for was not the Mentor herself once mentored?), turning a living person into an Undead Psychic Vampire.

The Mentor will come to teach her student, who is now the Neophyte Narc, many tools, not the least of which are:

- Love Bombing
- Early Consistency, Later Erraticism
- The Advanced Use of Taboo Deeds Made to Ensure a Crazy-Making Response
- Sexual Manipulation
- Hot-and-Cold Undulation Manipulation
- Small Lies to Divert from Big Lies
- It's All About the Response
- How to Use the Legal System to Punish Men
- How to Convincingly Make EVERY Man a Narcissist

And above all of these: How to Properly Devalue and Discard the Supply Who Won't Become the Quiet Man...

CHAPTER 6
A MAN'S SOCIAL MEDIA POLICY
FOR LATER-IN-LIFE LOVERS,
AND THE EARLY ONSET OF TABOOS

A note regarding the following section

The foundation of the background, levers, motives and assignable causes (with careful and ongoing proclamation that the ultimate, true, and final assignable cause is **CHOICE**, and thus freedom, and thus personal accountability) of the Psychic Femme Vampire has now been laid. The brooding, cold, calculated and unloved beauty who must feed on the vital and virile essence of masculinity is revealed. The Walking Dead devoid of empathy, consideration or regard for the success, wellbeing, growth or happiness of others is exposed. The One Who Venerates Self – imbalanced, unnatural and ungodly love of Self, as paramount above all – has been unveiled; let us transition from who she is into what she does and, more importantly, *what responses should be considered by the man trapped thereby.*

The upcoming chapter captures some examples of the intentional playbooks by the 'covert' female narcissist. The greater emphasis, however, or take-away from the reader, should be how men should consider acting, asserting and reclaiming their knighthood in a post-gender, post-truth world-gone-mad.

This isn't about her, male reader over thirty that has loved and lost, it is about *you*; your empathy, your intentional romantic routines and rituals, your commitment to communication, your softness, your accountability to actively listen, to provide, to cultivate, to serve and to protect.

Against the backdrop of falling in love with a monster (as so many have, and will, for *we like who we like, and there is no type)*, let gentlemanliness, knighthood and character be resurrected!

Social Media Scrying, and the Onset or 'Reeling in of the Prey'

Glaringly conspicuous it is that most relationships are born in this age via social media. All but gone are happenstance encounters at a bookstore, or the catching of a look of fancy whilst jogging in Central Park. Indeed, an adult is more likely to secure a first date with someone they've never seen in the flesh than attend a nervous, blush-filled coffee date with the one they've been gazing upon from three pews back at church for the past three months.

It is a Digital Dispensation, and the well-trained Psychic Vampire is an expert fisher in the lake of data and gigabytes. She knows at what ratios to 'like' your posts and pics, when to make a passing comment, how to flirt and lure in seven words or less. What masquerades as mysticism is actually analytics, algorithms and design.

The Vampire uses her mobile phone as a modern-day scrying bowl. She is watching, baiting and drawing you in. She knows what men fancy, how we respond – the path to rapid smitten and spellbound wonder.

In a healthy, self-actualized, mutually invested relationship, women will often muse how easy we are to manage. And they are not wrong. The rule of 3 Fs and 3 Sevens are really all women, who are far more complex than the counterparts the Lord has made for them, need to wield unlimited power (this is written in jest, but in jest, more truth than jest).

The 3 Fs to Satisfy Any Man:
1. Feed Him
2. Fuck Him
3. (Have) Fun (With) Him

Is it really that simple? Aye. This is one of the key secrets that women prior to the wave of destructive anti-family, anti-female, anti-human, anti-civilization feminism rocked the foundation of modern reality:

- The way to a man's heart really, actually and truly is through his stomach.
- Making a man feel desired sexually and being intimate with him often is paramount to a long and successful relatio ship – sex never, ever, ever being weaponized, or with malice withheld.
- Men truly and deeply disdain grumpy, uptight and cruel or mean partners. Women who keep it light, wield humor and engage men with silliness and mirth have the greatest chance for sustainable success.

What's more, the "3 Sevens", which represent exactly two minutes and twenty-two seconds of daily effort, will give a man a Holy Grail gulp of life-giving virility and joy, causing him to feel as the king in the amazing kingdom that is your family/relationship. Seven times per day, say these things to your man:

1. I love you
2. You're strong
3. You're handsome

Wielding these in all of their creative variants is easy, and they are of the deepest meaning, value and import to a man (especially when the man actually loves and adores his partner). Oh, how these secrets have supported men on days when they were afraid to come home after being terminated, having lost the big game, suffered failure or masked the private hurts that leaders mask! The suicides and despair saved by marvelous women wielding the power of edifying, well-placed words!

How much more dangerous, then, are these love-spells in the hands of a dark witch? A Vampire who uses them to build and manifest masculine energy, and then feed upon the supply of that which she gestated? She will admire you, celebrate your children with you, warmly applaud your shared accomplishments and begin acting as a steady 'quasi-girlfriend', even ere the first DM is sent.

Note that the Vampire:

- Is gorgeously beautiful
- Presents herself as conservative but a little witchy, a little hippie, and a little dark (this paradoxical and oxymoronical blend is what all men seek; let the philosophers and poets ponder, but none dispute!)
- Presents herself as understanding you, speaking your language, sharing your woes and views
- Presents herself as 'out of your league', yet likes you just the same

The feeling of digital euphoria is like a drug to men. It feels seductively intoxicating that she interacts with you in even slight measure. Without one handshake, one hug, one icebreaking glass of wine, she has you – over the internet.

Then one day, you really start to look at her page... and the ambiguity and concern begins.

From a timing perspective, the Vampire has already fanged you; the first drops of her poison have already integrated with and are parasitically absorbing your life essence. Even before the initial text or Direct Message (DM) is sent, there is a germ of concern, a tiny pea in the mattress, a fly-speck of warning.

It is at this point, before the man is fully overcome with loving the Vampire, that his will can still, with great difficulty, turn him away. Although this book advocates the opposite of the break-up and throw-away mania that is destroying the family unit and western civilization, this very early stage is an opportunity (maybe the only opportunity) to abort, move on to other online opportunities, and mitigate the pain of her bite.

But the euphoria outweighs the concern. And the concern is thus: it is unknown if she has a husband, serious boyfriend or partner. There are hints, but it could go either way.

The ambiguity is intentional.

Remember, the Vampire has been taught by her mistress or adept to commit ongoing, organized, intentional societal and cultural taboos. These inappropriate, off-putting or crazy-making practices are not done for their own sakes. Rather, they are done solely to beget *your response,* which will become the only thing remembered, focused upon and mercilessly judged:If your response is to 'put up with it' and do nothing, she will continue to commit the taboo in an effort to wear you out, feed upon you and relish in her easy achievement of the Quiet Man. Under this scenario, she will enjoy serially cheating on you and feed on the energy of your 'knowing but not quite knowing' or 'keeping your head down' or being 'lost in scotch' as she berates and betrays you. This Quiet Man may be discarded quickly, or conversely used for years and years, depending upon the energy supply provided.

If your response is harsh or full of righteous indignation, she will feast on the fighting, gorging herself on the conflict. You will be made the monster for your 'controlling, narcissistic responses' to her taboo behavior, and a cycle of outrage, fighting and making up will keep her well-fed for months or years until she, declaring her full victimhood, suddenly discards this version of the now worn-out and pale version of the Quiet Man. (In other scenarios, the once strong, proud warrior simply gives up and becomes the first example above.)

Taboo is EVERYTHING for the Psychic Vampire. And ambiguity about another man in the picture is always her first, and often favorite, taboo during the identification and hunting of her prey.

Let us never become what we oppose as men. Let us never visit upon our partners, prospects and women what we have suffered in these heart-wrenching scenarios. Let there be no taboo.

Let us, as Knights, establish the following Social Media Policy for Later-in-Life Love:

1. **State your relationship status clearly** – if you have a girl-friend, fiancée or wife, it should take zero clicks for women online to see this.

2. **For romance, balance your volume of posts** – it becomes a patently over-compensatory indicator of a bad relationship to post pictures of every walk you take, every meal you

eat, every time you shop. No one cares to see your romance unfold in detail nine times a day. It looks desperate – or conversely, it imposes your 'look at me, look at me' relationship into the faces of thousands of viewers who may be struggling in their own private lives.

However, the opposite is also unhealthy. Posting nothing, ever, sends the message not of privacy, but of misleading availability. You are proud of your fiancée, girlfriend or wife, and there is nothing wrong in proclaiming that to the world, periodically. Celebrate her achievements at work; post a picture of her caught laughing and enjoying life, or snuggling a puppy.

The cyber-world should clearly know that:

1. You are hers
2. You value her
3. You are her biggest fan – but without chronically putting it in everyone's face.

The by-product of this is that the privacy and intimacy of your love is protected, your friends get to be part of your romance with limits, and other women fully know that they have no chance with you: avoiding the taboo of you pursuing one woman when, behind the scenes, you have another.

- **Avoid Social Media Posts To Her, Entirely** – couples that wish each other a "Good morning" from page to page tell the world that the relationship is in trouble and that you have to do in public what you obviously can't do privately – communication. You have text messages, video conferences or, better, the resurrection of the art of han written notes for such things, and these are the much preferred medium.

- **Never, Ever, Ever Post Anything Negative or Gossipy About Your Partner on Social Media** – conflict will occur. Dynamic, outgoing, passionate individuals argue; it will happen. When it does, seek the support of a small (male only) circle of confidants. Vent, complain, listen to objective advice

Then restore yourself quickly to your lady love, never letting the sun set on your anger.

Do not disrespect her, or disgrace your team, by airing your laundry in a forum so volatile and potentially vile as the World Wide Web. This simply should not happen, and often cannot, when the offense is committed, be undone. In addition to embarrassing her and demonstrating instability and immaturity, it invites infidelity, with many women looking to fully breach the fracture you've revealed, breaking you up entirely, and *stealing you*. Much adultery is engendered through complaining, belittling or defaming one's partner online.

For the Modern-Day Knight, honor her above all else, and when angry with her or in the storm of disagreement, double down and honor her more. For storms give way to bright sunrises and new days, but internet posts are archived forever.

CHAPTER 7
"NO, HE'S NOT JUST HER GAY ROOMMATE": THE GREEN TABOO

As the courting accelerates, the prey's judgement proportionally diminishes. Awareness and sound decision-making, logic and reason, are displaced by emotion and desire.

Outside of the sun rising tomorrow in the east, and setting again when evening comes in the west, there is no truth more firm, neither maxim more universal and true than this: the small-town Femme Vampire has another man, and often a plurality of men. Each of these are ambiguous, and none clear, especially to one another. She will not fully be able to hide her statedly awkward 'other guy situation'; neither does she want to. Through the ambiguity of her relationship status online (and other strategies), her aim is to at first sloppily conceal – remember, she grossly misuses the notion of being an 'introvert' and will simply cite 'privacy' for her cover-up of any inappropriate situation – then reveal that there is in fact another (at least one) man in her life. Were the matter evaluated when her target was in his right mind, he would here RUN or at minimum, bow out gracefully. Alas, already bewitched by spells cast through the mobile device medium (or, if she concealed this taboo long enough, perhaps a first physical encounter), he can no more turn away from his attraction to her than can the moth flee the flame.

She has intentionally orchestrated this taboo for two defined purposes:

- To actively demonstrate her narcissism – namely that whatever feels good, no matter how viewed by cultural or societal norms, she will do. She will do it with a quiet, falsely shy resolve, then shriek in victimized howls if the taboo is contested. She wants to shriek and howl, and this taboo is her preferred pretext for the same.

• To provoke you into greenest jealousy. For jealousy is the rage of men, and the rage of men is her supply. Your righteous and just jealousy will be fanned and fumed until you at last act out inappropriately: perhaps by hollering, in verbal dispute, or violating her 'privacy'. You then will be the 'controlling jerk', the 'abuser', for not being blissfully acquiescent to her 'arrangements' with another man/men.

Once the anger begets an untoward response, she will feast upon the chaos, sadness and strife. When at last you yield, submitting to her outrageous arrangement with another male that has known her *biblically*, the residue is now well en route to your new reality as the Quiet Man; the defeated, soulless fellow, confused and tired. The beleaguered, castrated eunuch who shares his girlfriend. Defeated and desperate, increasingly insecure (for you are literally sharing your woman with another man) and no longer your confident, relaxed self, you exist now only to be energized periodically again with the coming of the next taboo.

The *Green*, or Jealousy, Taboo takes many forms. Some example scenarios include:

Living with the Ex for Financial Reasons
This taboo is concealed with lies and misdirection during the 'social media' or even early dating phase and, when revealed, is done so with a feigned sorrow that she was not more upfront about her living situation.

Typically, but not exclusively, the Psychic Vampire will slowly attempt to soften the shock of the taboo by putting her ex/roommate down in a double-dealing effort to build you up.

As modern knights, we must never put others down to elevate ourselves or our partners. Nor shall we give space for others to put other men down in an effort to elevate ourselves. For know this: if she is putting him down today, you will be the object of tomorrow's insults to the next guy. Your partner's value stands on its own merits, as does yours. The appropriate attitude when discussing an ex with our current partner should be one of neighborly fondness, neutrality measured with kindness, and no more. Such discussions should be on an 'only when absolutely required' basis and most rare.

In an age where common sense is wanting and truth itself under furious assault, what was once plainly known and accepted must here be memorialized. It is patently inappropriate for a man to cohabitate with a prior lover. As men, we would not like our wife or girlfriends to do this to us; let therefore the Golden Rule prevent the Green Taboo in our treatment of her.

Her first pass at nudging you in the Quiet Man direction will be through grey haziness about the relationship with her 'roommate'. Common half-truths and misnomers may include:

- Timeline fuzziness: "We broke up six years ago – well, three, but I was emotionally done with him at six..."
- "Just roommates with a ring": "Yes, we are technically married, but we stopped having sex years ago and just function as roommates until we sell this darn house."
- Sexual orientation: "All of my girlfriends told me he's gay, and I really believe he is."
- Irrelevant information about *his* relationship status: *"Don't worry, he has a girlfriend."*

Her story will shift around, bobbling and toggling until it settles on the final narrative that you will have to either 'like or lump'; any protest or objection to the situation constitutes, in the mind of the Vampire, narcissism and control – in a remarkable twist of logic, **by you!**

The difficult reality is that if your new, super-sexy, professional, sorta hippie, kinda dark yet conservative and lady-like dream babe lives with her ex-boyfriend or spouse... they are sleeping together. The reason you go to bed at night feeling crazy, unsettled and disquieted in your soul, haunted by persistent thoughts of *him* sneaking into her room for late-night jaunts, is *because he is sneaking into her room for late-night jaunts.*

Unlike the Post-Modernists, the Relativists and the Humanists, the worldview put forth here conforms to that which is real where reality is concerned. Her taboo, her living with him whilst forming a relationship with you, will be a root and source of manifold miseries over the ensuing months and years.

A Close Friend from the Military

Another form of the Green Taboo may manifest in the form of a close male friend from her military career/association. She will cite various factors that contribute to her collection of these types of men, which might include:

- The military is 'like a family', where strong bonds form in the flower of youth. These relationships are lifelong, and gender is irrelevant.
- Many who join the military have troubled family histories and become 'adopted' into more stable environments. In this regard, the male military friend is viewed as 'closer than a brother'.
- When the Vampire was being 'abused' by her narcissistic husband, this male friend, who was first his friend, was there for her, and became her friend.

Regardless of the veracity of these factors, it is the behavior of the pair, not their origin story, that becomes the taboo:

- He wrestles with her and engages in overtly flirtatious 'horseplay' in unacceptable volumes and at wildly unacceptable times and occasions.
- He constantly talks about sexual relations in an overly familiar, creepy way.

- He makes jokes referencing sexual interactions in the past... with her... in your presence.
- His conduct, outside of the sex category, is forward, vulgar and inappropriate.
- He has territorial, primal control over her like a protective sibling, constantly finding creative ways to let you know that 'he was there first' and is more important than you, or any of her past or future partners.
- He is given a free pass. The way he treats her would be decried as 'narcissism' or 'abuse', were it committed by another man (especially you), but it's somehow 'ok' or even 'cute' because it's her military friend.

This taboo brings about great embarrassment, as every onlooker in your circle sees the inappropriateness of the relationship, but struggles to break silence over the matter for fear of disparaging a veteran.

As a Modern Knight, when we enter into a new relationship, we are accountable for appropriate conduct with our friends of the other gender. It is not the friendship with a high-school, military or long-time family friend that is wrong or immoral, for surely there are a multitude of lifelong friendships that edify, encourage and add great value to marriage. However, any female friend that chooses to

- Be lewd
- Intentionally make your new girlfriend uncomfortable
- Draw most conversations to sex
- Chronically hint at any 'hook-ups', 'one-night stands' or impulsive choices in youth involving the two of you, or
- Create mental images of you with other women (for she knows your past) in the presence of your new partner

is actually not a friend – rather a lonely villain seeking to destroy your relationship and hoard you for themselves. An actual friend would discern your embryonic love and developing adoration for your new partner, reel in the locker-room banter, and make every effort to see your girlfriend respected and your relationship healthy and growing.

Again, through application of the Golden Rule to avoid the Green Taboo, you have every right to assert that your girlfriend or fiancée likewise ensures that boundaries are friendly and clear with her military friend. Whether she has known him for a month, a year or three decades is irrelevant. You and your Team come first, not the lewd guy showing cock pics and flatulating in front of your fiancée, who thinks it's ok because "they've been friends since the 90s".

An Obnoxious and Lewd Homosexual Best Friend

The Psychic Femme Vampire finds sinister elation in this taboo. Remember, her objective is to create a distressed *response* from her Quiet Man. She drains him in two ways:

1. Via strife and conflict, which produces adrenaline and negative energy. This type of energy is renewable.
2. Through downtrodden, extreme quiet, which produces the sweet elixirs of submission and life-depleting energy. This type of energy is fixed and not renewable.

By sharp contrast, couples in a healthy, loving, edifying relationship where they seek first the needs of their partner understand the importance of consistency, love rituals, humor, teamwork and grace. They also manifest, manufacture, and yes, in many ways consume the energy of their partners as well. The difference is that this energy is infectious, warm, fun, life-giving, and mutually enjoyed with every hand-hold, every wink, every foot massage, every long walk, every quiet moment of contemplation after a favorite film, every long hug after loss or failure, every well-placed and perfectly timed complement. This type of energy is positive and renewable.

The nature of this particular taboo very much focuses on the second form of energy drain cited above. She will seek the most sordid, lewd gay men she can conjure, become their 'fag hag', then turn them loose on you.

For, given the environs of Cancel Culture and Political Correctness, who would dare to utter a word when her homosexual friend:

- talks about her current period in vivid, first-hand detail to include flow amount and consistency?
- joins her in the washroom when she is urinating?
- describes every thrust of his most recent anal sex encounter?

The raising of one sentence of objection to his crass, untoward behavior with your girlfriend or spouse would of course render you:

- A Nazi
- A bigot
- A neanderthal

Only in a world gone insane would the person crying "The barn is on fire!" be branded the arsonist. But alas, we live in such a time.

Would you, the Modern-Day Knight, discuss bathroom habits and goings-on with a female friend, regardless of her sexual orientation? Nay. Delve into details about sexual congress using loud metaphors with the open intent of 'shock and awe'? Also nay. Permit another woman (or any person) to watch you pee? Never.

Her friend is not *just one of the girls,* regardless of whether he or they want to suspend reality and declare it so. Sexual orientation is not a license for taboo, neither for crudeness, nor disrespect.

There ought to be no special treatments and *cartes blanches* for rudeness on the merits of which group someone identities with. Right and wrong extend to the individual, and you are not a Nazi for thinking this way; indeed, they are Nazis for thinking that one group is exempt for that which another group is accountable for.

The irony of this effective taboo will be that, behind closed doors, the Psychic Vampire will confide in you fiercely anti-gay sentiments. Citing that she just 'feels badly for him' or 'met him through work and can't get rid of him', she will bash the gay fellow with unrivaled disgust, hate and pretense.

This is a ploy; this is a trap. Do not engage. Do not participate.

Modern Knight, love all people. Give no place to hate. The gay gentleman will be in her circle long after you have been devalued and thrown away. She is only provoking you to negative discourse about him so that she can weaponize it later. We do not care who people hump, love, or spend their time with. It's none of our business. What we care about is that every individual is respectful, polite, and edifies strong, committed relationships.

The Nerd Friend That Could Never Have Her

This scenario is the most difficult, as it will pull at *your* heartstrings. Under this strategy, the Vampire collects a male friend who is very nice, very decent, a little weird (but let's face it – weird is cool, and you're a little weird too!), somewhat physically weak (he could not harm her in a fight, and at school she likely protected him from bullies), fashionably challenged, and for the better part a benign mess.

Whereas the ex-roommate IS bedding down your woman, and whereas the military friend is *probably* doing the same, this person is benign and is NOT having a physical affair with her. Rather, he is engaged in an ongoing emotional, spiritual and mental affair.

He is the one she confides in over a meal.

He is the one she texts when you have a quarrel.

He is the one who hangs out with her sister, her parents, her girlfriends.

She can say anything to him.

Though men posture as too tough to protest or even acknowledge this, emotional betrayal may be, in many ways, worse than physical cheating. Anything that belongs in the parameter and boundary of an exclusive relationship that is given, shared or engaged in with someone who is not your exclusive partner *is cheating*.

Her use of the 'nerd that could never have her' is as damaging and hurtful to him as it is to you. The Nerd typically honors boundaries, respects you, and is fighting a war within his soul – for he is in love with her. She gives him the scraps and crumbs, and he cannot turn from them. So, he engages.

Her hopes are that she will push you (this taboo is a long game, not a sprint) to finally, one day, boil over and unleash pent-up anger about her ongoing sharing of your personal lives and dealings with the Nerd. The very instant a jealous protest leaves your lips, she will feast. You will be branded a jealous maniac for the sum of the relationship: for what kind of man other than a monster or maniac could possibly protest her innocent friendship with the Nerd?

Fearing this, most men simply suffer her collection of inappropriate, or inappropriately conducted, relationships with men and suppress their emotion (and words), giving her the pleasure of drinking the static submission of the Quiet Man.

Your partner will have men in her life. If she wanted to be with them, she surely could have done so already. Support and encourage healthy relationships; be a stable and secure leader. If there are issues, discuss boundaries and solutions and strongly avoid accusations (that are 98% unfounded). Women are far more loyal and monogamous than men, and very, very few women are Psychic Vampires or Werewolves. The overwhelming majority of women will identify, squash and manage the above scenarios rapidly. If you have been through the crucible of enduring these intentional taboos, be most careful not to impose the weight and carrying of your baggage by your next travel partner...

CHAPTER 8
LOVE BOMBING AND THE CONSISTENCY YO-YO

Although there is a collective fatigue over the chronic, droning overuse and misuse of psychobabble phrases, there are a few that are on point and have no better synonym – "love bombing" being chief amongst these.

Love bombing is best described through examples of its outworking. During the early phases of courtship with a Psychic Vampire, there will be an intentional blitzkrieg of:

- Small, extremely thoughtful and meaningful gifts
- Establishment of love rituals
- Doting and compliments
- Love notes
- Demonstrative subject matter expertise in the arts and nuance of Communication

These, along with friendship, physical intimacy and otherworldly levels of expert communication, become the foundation of the relationship.

When she is shopping with her girlfriends, she sees a little tie clip that you might adore. Although the outing was about her now-declining time with her besties (for by this point her time is consumed with seeing you, and making you feel as the center of her universe), she manages to steal away from them and score you the love token.

She's quickly learned your favorite color and finds quirky, zany ways to incorporate it into inexpensive yet priceless crafts or handmade gifts.

You've co-discovered your mutual love of coffee, and she's established a ritual of 'Wednesday recommendations': broadening your morning brew horizons, enlightening your world to a vast, unexplored wilderness of wondrous beans, aromas and giddy, caffeine-induced jitters. She also helped you learn about Stevia.

Her attentiveness is unrivaled, and she's learned that you love holding hands. Thus she has mastered nine kinds of handhold techniques, giving each of them names, engaging in bellowing laughter as she clasps, knots, pinky-ties and otherwise makes love to you through the congress of fingers and palms.

The foundation of your love is as granite; the cornerstone laid with deep friendship, deeper respect, and romance limitless. The prey could not be happier, neither fly higher than at the apex of this cometary rain of gooey greatness.

She knows this, and the shower of sun and rainbows is about to turn, seemingly in an instant, to icicles and anesthesia. For, when the timing aligns with her strategy, she intentionally cracks that foundation with a jackhammer called 'withholding' and a mallet called 'honeymoon phase.'

Love bombing has at its core the willful intent of presenting yourself as romantic, affectionate and wildly passionate, then withdrawing, down-throttling or ceasing entirely the acts, gifts and rituals for the purpose of creating longing, desperation, doubt, strife, worry, graspings for control and then, ironically, submission to a new state. *The Quiet Man state.*

Longing.

Desperation.

Doubt.

Strife.

Worry.

Grasping for control.

Submission.

Each of these is essential for supply of the Psychic Femme Vampire.

If she used to tell you that you're handsome 793 times a day for the first three months of the relationship and now it's 0 times per day, you are being love bombed. (Note – or, if she's not a Psy Vamp, she simply is no longer into you, which is a different struggle and outside the scope of this tome).

If the handwritten notes that filled your heart (and the hollowed-out treasure box concealed within the shell of a book that houses your collection of them) have been replaced with lazily penned text messages, or worse, nothing, then you are being love bombed.

If you were gifted five hats in the first five months, then no hats in the next five – love bomb.

If you came together oft to savor every sip of a new blend of the coffee, tea or wine you discovered and the sacred act has suddenly been replaced with her not caring whether the morning brew be arabica, robusta or hot tar, she has dropped the love bomb upon you.

The Vampire has a ready-made defense, should you confront the overt shift in affection, the clear change in the pace, tempo and feel of the relationship:

"You're keeping score."

"You think you're entitled to it."

"You're controlling me."

The reality is that you are doing none of these things. Rather:

"I am a thinking person and observant and can patently tell that there is a material change. I'm not nitpicking; I'm seeing what is plain and obvious."

"I am not entitled to anything save consistency."

"I am controlling nothing; I am trying to understand why there has been a change."

"Love loves!"

Love bombing is lethal, cruel, visiting a devastation second only perhaps to outright infidelity. It is a category of no return; the death of what was, and what can never be again.

Consider. The moment you shine a spotlight on withdrawn affection, gift-giving or ritual, no future act of affection, gift-giving, or ritual can be as it was.

If you have accused her wrongly and she is *not* love bombing you, then she will, in the future, feel that she is performing those acts of love by debt or obligation, instead of through the joy of *wanting to*. Unfounded complaints and criticisms are both romance- and love-killers, even in otherwise healthy relationships.

If you have made your stand and your expression of concern is the correct diagnosis, then she will engage in the torture of mechanical or rote romance, followed by more withholding, followed by more 'recovery of romance', followed by more withholding – until when at last you are numb and exhausted, you wholly forget the good season of 'love bombs' that drew you so deeply into love with her in the first place.

The nanosecond that the Prey opens his mouth about love bombing, or about material changes in her effort, the season of pure, real, and fairytale romance ends – forever. (The fact that it was never real to begin with does nothing to offset the agony and loss of *what it was.*)

This writer does not endorse or promote breaking up as the quick, 'canned' solution, neither choosing never to forgive, nor discarding and devaluing individuals you love; even if the one you love is a monster that is syphoning your soul on purpose. But alas, know that if you are able to stay, it can never be as it was.

If you are able to respectfully assert your position, communicate it clearly, redefine your standards and expectations and 'stay', then do so with encouragement and grace. However, the categories of:

- Gifts
- Affection
- Notes/unique communication methods
- Love Rituals

must be drastically adjusted with respect to expectations. In this regard, your relationship will be average, lack that which is special and unique, and bend the knee to the frightening idea that active love doth fade and that honeymoon seasons are not only real, but acceptable.

Most probably the exposure of her love bombing then gives way to the lying and cheating she needs to feed upon you, and she will destroy, devalue and leave you in the end anyway.

The greater focus for the Modern Knight is not how to undo her love bombing. Rather, it is what the man[6] can do *next time* and what lessons can be gleaned in how he treats future partners. We cannot control how others treat us; we can only control how we respond and how we in turn, choose to pass that wisdom forward into how we treat others and our future selves.

First, talk about consistency and worldview early in the relationship. As you find yourself in the gooey tempest of wondrous new romance, do well to pause and incorporate thoughtful and kind discussions about whether you and she are a 'phase couple' or a 'consistency couple'. This type of discourse is very difficult for us hopeless romantics – but recall, the primary audience of this book is men above thirty who have failed in love or been fanged by the Femme Vamp. A young couple in the spring of youth need not over-diagnose such things, neither dwell upon them. Instead, just **be consistent with your lass!**

Second, never, ever do to another woman what the Femme Vampire did to you. The reality is that men love bomb women far, far more frequently than the reverse. Although this is mostly driven by laziness and not malevolence, her hurt is the same; her pain cares not for your motive. Where a man may not be looking to 'yo-yo and destroy her', he may be practicing a softer form of using love bombing to win her, then settle into his lazy approach to loving her once won.

---

6   Note that there appears to be very little nuance or gender-centric considerations/differences for this particular tool of the "Covert Narc", and the same can be said for women on the mend from a male love-bomber as well

Be none of these things! Use your experience and survival as a careful lesson of 'what not to do' to others. Do not compel your new partner to carry the Vampire's luggage, nor impose your past abuse on your new partner, but DO harken unto lessons learned and remember that your actions towards your new lady-love are very, very serious and impact her (and her loved ones, family, children, etc.) very seriously.

Third, actively practice consistent love by choice. What you do in week one, do also, or better, when she is seventy.

The Modern Knight should be in an accountability and 'service as leadership' mindset and tempo for the whole of his relationship (and life). You are accountable to her. She deserves your respect; and nowhere does respect manifest more positively than in the area of consistency. Once you have learned what she likes, do it. And do it consistently.

Note that this is not about rote mechanics and assembly-line love. We all change through the process of time. Therefore this principle does not always mean doing the exact same thing you did at twenty-five (though it well could; the Modern Knight must read this situation). It's about investing the same vigor, effort, newness and verve towards her at fifty-five that you invested at twenty-five.

Love is hard work. Do not drop love bombs that crater her soul. Rather, love her with uplifting, never-changing showers of love that feed, water, and edify her.

CHAPTER 3
THE ART OF ERRATICISM

The Vampire has been mentored, as stated afore, and what distinguishes her from a regular, everyday 'bad partner' is the element of *intent*, the execution of methodology. She is a priestess, and her religion is the destruction of anything masculine. Hers is as much a sociopathic outrage against the nuclear family, the church, and the community as it is a relationship dysfunction. She loathed her perceived imprisonment of small-town America – Ma, Pa and apple pie – then the soldier boy broke her heart, and now the whole of western civilization must pay.

You must pay...

After laying you to waste with the giving (and subsequent taking away) of love bombs, the next stage in her plan to make of you the Quiet Man is erraticism. She has barraged you with gifts, love rituals, passionate movie-level lovemaking, poetry, and late nights become early mornings, her mere presence filling you with the energy and verve of 10,000 suns.

And now the syringe of her fangs must puncture the swell of your neck, imbibing her fill of that energy.

This she will do via two primary vehicles:

Her false declarations that personality type ('Introvert') exempts her from being accountable to you... or anything or anyone else.

She will be erratically and spontaneously mean to her prey, typically following a (now diminishing in frequency) well-placed love bomb.

She's Not an Introvert, She's Cruel and Cold

When the key indicators of love bombing, then withholding, then erraticism are protested (no matter how diplomatically or gently stated), false and self-righteous declarations of being an 'empath' and 'introvert' will follow.

Mind you, in the formative period of the relationship she was:

- Outgoing
- Full of verve
- Consistent
- Social

If personality types exist at all (and again, this writer cautions against any school of thought that abdicates from the individual their Free Will, Personal Accountability and Choice, and thus liberty), then *actual* introverts, or those predisposed to introversion, ought be insulted above all others that the Covert Narc appropriates his or herself to the predisposition.

Those who identify with introverted leanings are, for the better part, overwhelmingly:

- Consistent in their exchange of energy with others
- Kind in their assertion for space and alone time
- Wildly romantic, although it may manifest differently than those who are more outgoing
- Still attentive to the thoughts, feelings and views of others.

The Femme Vampire is none of these things. Her attestation of introversion is rather:

"I will be nice when I want to, and rude when I feel like it. If you challenge this, you are not respecting that I am an introvert."

"I will be making out with you one moment in the laundry room and then disappear in an instant, only to be found scowling at nothing in particular in our room, for I am an introvert."

"I will make plans with my girlfriends, only to cancel them at the last moment without cause, for I am an introvert. And later that night, when I am home with you, I will blame you for the broken plans, for I am an introvert."

"I will stop responding to texts randomly, for I am an introvert."

"I will not only stop responding to the little (or big) thoughtful things you do, but I will slowly start to mock them as 'too much', for I am an introvert."

"I will be cold, I will be cruel, for I am an introvert."

Whatever view one holds on personality types and other forms of determinism, there is no exemption for abusive, destructive or hurtful behavior. The Femme Psychic Vampire has free will, and choice, and she is choosing erratic behavior to break down her prey, to cause turmoil (which feeds her), submission (which supplies her), then your withdrawal (which justifies her cheating on you), and ultimately, your full devaluing and discarding (leaving you for the next one).

Inversion of Male Abuse; She Buys You Flowers Then Slaps You

Most of what the world calls 'narcissism' is very similar in attributes and outworking, regardless of gender; and a monster is a monster.

However, the genders are different. Men and women differ; physically, emotionally, chemically, and spiritually. Male and female have different offices in this, the human experience, and were designed to complement, support and synergize one with another as seen in the Sacred Geometry that cries out its witness of the marvelous handiwork of God throughout the whole of Creation.

Because of this truth, there are nuances and gender-centric differences where perversion, abuse and malevolence is concerned.

And although there are far more males roaming the countryside, drunk on power and self, brimming with control issues and given to wanton bullying of their partners, when the Narc is a *real Narc*, and a woman, she is more sinister tenfold than her male peers.

And although she can be as physically abusive as men (to be covered elsewhere), making every possible excuse for why her prey's provocation caused her to bite him, strike him with a candlestick or even use closed fists for punches and pounding, her '*buying you flowers then slapping you'* is metaphoric for the unique way in which she intentionally pours out the good times as a manipulative pretext for the bad.

The male 'abuses first, feigns regret second', asserting his misplaced power and abuse of position over his wife or girlfriend. Seeing her browbeaten, defeated, deflated or disassociated, he withdraws so she can replenish, then is nice for a spell (buying her flowers) that he might feed again.

The Femme Vampire set-up is precisely opposite. She will lull her prey into a sense of peace, of relaxed (yet paradoxically high-octane) romantic energy gelatin. Swimming as king of his new-found realm of the heart, once he is calm and confident, she strikes.

Disarm.

Shock.

Reaction.

Confusion.

She took the bouquet out of your hands as you were beholding their fragrance, and proceeded to beat you with them. This is the *Art of Erraticism.*

Befuddled by her diminishing acts of intentional and thoughtful affection. Nervous at the diminishing of love notes and collarbone butterfly kisses, now the prey senses the weight of a very real transition (often only three to six months removed from his perceived blissfully gooey love-topia), for not only is she withholding love and inflicting pain via erratic 'hot-cold' behavior, but she is now actually lashing out at you.

The list of 'nevers' and 'thankfully that kind of thing never happens in our relationship' has given way to simply trying to survive random criticisms, coldness, and name-calling.

A man confused, on edge and losing confidence is tempted to respond, which is the aim of the vampiric artist. *For it is always about the response. By the response a man will be judged. She is an adept and knows this...* She wants to make of the man a yo-yo and she the string. As he undulates in crazy-making confusion, he is primed for the next phase in his metamorphosis from virile, fun, outgoing, self-actualized gentleman to a grey walking skeleton of emasculation; the Quiet Man.

On to the next phase of increasingly bizarre taboos...

CHAPTER 10
THE ADVANCED USE OF TABOOS AND DEEDS
TO ENSURE A CRAZY-MAKING RESPONSE
ACT 1
THE FAMILY BED

Until now, there has been a defined, structured and intentional order of events; a pattern and sequence to the small-town Psychic Vampire's pursuit, capture, and preparation of her meal. Now the oven heat in earnest will be turned to the 'high position', as the seasoning and marination of the meat that is your heart is completed. The time to cook you is at hand.

The order, with some variability, is summarized thusly:

- Wondrous, soul-mate-level beginnings, but... something off-putting or untoward about other males (the ex-roomate, the gay friend, etc.). *The green taboo from the start*
- The blitzkrieg of love bombs and the craterous desolation of their cessation
- The 'buying you flowers' (the brief reappearance of the love bomb for which he so desperately yearns) followed by the slap, or expert execution of erraticism

What follows next will *not* be in any definable order, neither follow a pattern that can be assessed through predictive analytics. Indeed, some of what follows may have occurred in parallel or as garnish to the green taboo, love bombing or art of erraticism – but its frequency, intensity and impact is now surging this side of the preliminary strategies.

Henceforth, the preamble has concluded and the man is in the actual storm – and who can know the whims and fancy of a cyclone?

Her investing in your love bank has diminished by this point to such a low level that the past glory (although only a few months ago) seems distant and unattainable. Self-doubt takes hold and inner queries abound: 'Was it ever real?' and 'Maybe we were broken from the beginning?' or 'Maybe my expectations are too high and this is my fault...'

Regardless of what the Psy Vamp does, the Modern Knight owns his response. She is seeking to make of you a Quiet Man, and your job is to fight and ultimately slay him. Your battle is not with her, it is with your responses – which you own. When the Quiet Man attempts to take over your inner voice, give no place to him, take up the microphone in your own head and rather let the Modern Knight retort resolutely:

Inner Question	The Answer of a Modern-Day Knight
Was it EVER real?	Yes, it was real. She chose to be awesome before, and she, via her free will, is choosing to be horrible now.
Were we broken from the beginning?	No, you were not broken from the beginning (save that she is a Vampire hell-bent on turning you into an alcoholic cadaver that sits in a corner and stares despondently into space while she fornicates and humiliates you as she fancies. Thus, your current relationship disposition is by design). It actually WAS romance-novel or rom-com-movie kind of love. Such love does exist, and you would be fool to let this monster rob you of thinking otherwise.
Are my expectations too high? Is this my fault?	No! Your expectations should be as lofty as that standard of excellence you set for yourself with respect to your personal accountability to your partner. If your standard is to be legendary, thoughtful and spectacularly gooey to her, then settle for nothing less for yourself!

Moreover, if the reader finds himself in the eye of the following (or similar) storms, knowing the paralyzing weight of daily lose-lose scenarios: snip out the above table from these pages, hide it in your journal, read it privily and shout it aloud when the Vampire is away!

This taboo only applies to the Femme Vamp who, by accident, has brought a child into this fallen and her sinister world.

For the Femme Vampire hates western civilization's precepts of the nuclear family. By extension, she hates the Judeo-Christian worldview of womanhood. And womanhood cannot be divorced from its highest calling: motherhood. Thus, by further extension, the Energy Bloodsucker hates children without respect of persons – including her own.

Alas, should she have offspring, the lad or lass will be a useful pawn, else an annoyance.

Remember, her veneer is *Soccer Mom but Sexy, New-Age Hipster* in vibe, *conservative* in attire and physical appearance. This disguise demands that she be a devoted mother, tirelessly committed to providing for her home and protecting the child from the supposedly toxic talons of her narcissistic, deadbeat ex-husband.

That's the narrative. That's the playbook.

Just as she, under the guidance of her long-barren mentor, has consumed every article ever penned about Personality Type and Narcissistic Personality Disorder, she also has PhD-level command of every nouveau concept connected to modernity's concept of 'motherhood'. Like a cloud without water, she knows all the tag-lines, but is bankrupt of natural affection. So fluent in the vernacular is she that her peer groups and work acquaintances see her as a self-sacrificing, desperately devoted and woebegone professional single mother 'doing the very best she can'.

But the world doth not live with her as, by this stage, you do... and you know better.

While she is making brownies for the 'Wednesday Mother-Daughter Craft Night', organizing rides and driving ten miles out of her way to make sure her child's less financially fortunate friend can make the event, you stumble upon literature in the kitchen drawer which explores abandoning her child to a life spent absent from Mom and Dad in military school.

The dichotomies are extreme. She rarely hugs or holds her little girl, but declares her love for her 'in other ways'. With the softest disposition, she gently practices the following:

- Letting the child choose to eat pizza and pop tarts for every meal
- Letting the child dominate the TV viewing schedule for the entire household
- Letting the child decide his/her own bed-time and bed-time routine
- Letting the child run the home
- Treating the child like a peer instead of... like a child

Such things are NOT love – rather its inversion. By treating the child as an adult – providing no boundaries, no teaching, no foundation – she ensures that they never become an adult. These things benefit not the child; they benefit the lazy parent, who is too selfish to raise the babes up in the way they ought to. Child-rearing is difficult work that requires grace, sacrifice, humor, and a flow of unyielding and unconditional love.

But this isn't a Parenting Book. A myriad of those fill the shelves and cyberstores.

The reality is that she does none of the above when she is alone with the child. Rather, she does them when her prey is with her: a set-up that will later disrupt and distress him, and thus feed her.

When it is just she and her child home alone, it looks more like this:

- "Eat whatever you want, I'm too busy for this shit"
- "Go to your room and watch whatever, but stay out of my space (I'm an Introvert)"
- "Go to bed whenever the hell you want to, I'm tired of hassling you about it and have important meetings in the morning"

- "You don't run this home – I will send you right back to your dad."

This all inevitably leads to the ten-year-old girl, whose entire life has been the yo-yo of undulating guilt and reward *(stop complaining, this poor lass has been through it her whole life, nine months of it isn't so bad)* to greatly look forward to you being there. After all, you are:

- Fun
- Soft
- Respectful
- Will invest in play, in art, in projects with her
- Parental. She is not your child, and you respect boundaries, but you are at least a leadership presence in the home.
- You love her mom with a relentless shiny energy that illuminates the home with merry. When a man loves a mother, it flows through the home, even if the mother is a devil.
- You are the neighborhood 'cool dad'.

The Psy Vamp wants the daughter to like you more than she reveres her own mother. Then she can run her taboo playbooks to create tension, awkwardness and dysfunction amongst you. This becomes a feast of energy for the hungry nightstalker!

One of the primary ways this is established is through habitual co-sleeping with a child who is far, far too old not to be in her own bed. And the bed not her own is YOUR bed, meaning that you too are expected to co-sleep with a young child.

This taboo, this disgustingly weird scenario where a 200lb man is in the same bed with a ten or eleven-year-old female child (that he did not sire) is immoral, wrong and destructive on too many levels to here enumerate, but outside and behind these, the primary reason the Psy Vamp does this is because she knows that the nighttime romantic routine and ritual is of paramount importance to a healthy couple. Disturbing the way your night ends assures that your morning will open 'off', and that your relationship will erode.

If you fight and protest, you are the jerk turning away a scared young child – a narcissist and an abuser. If you say nothing as night after night passes without intimacy, snuggling, making out and watching your favorite TV series with popcorn or a glass of wine, then you are the Quiet Man. A weakling. And no woman wants a weak man...

The bedtime routine is foundational, it is core, it is key to living and thriving as One Flesh.

- When the stressors of the day have concluded, your bedtime routine and love ritual is your time (not the children's time, not the mobile devices' or your buddies' time) to decompress, vent, and actively listen to one another.
- You are accountable to your partner to send him/her into a blissful, peaceful and restful night.
- You are accountable to learn what she likes, and rub her feet or massage the muscles that have knotted up thanks to a day of 'working and momming' all day long. And if that massage is wanted every night from 9:15pm to 9:44pm then you, Modern Knight, provide that act of love and service from 9:15pm to 9:44pm... every night.
- The bedtime ritual is where you talk. Where you really hold one another and *talk*.
- "Waiting to plan a day on the day is a day too late." As a team, the nighttime ritual is where you collaborate on how to attack the following day so that you 'hit the ground running.'
- Lovemaking should be very frequent, random, spontaneous and full of diversity and creativity. However, the 'opportunity' for lovemaking is clearly most often during the nighttime or bedtime routine; this is known between the couple and need not be mentioned or 'planned'.

Nighttime is adult time.

Actual, real nightmares, illnesses, or spontaneous popcorn nights notwithstanding (for THESE are the legitimate reasons that warm, loving and well-rounded adults and/or parents DO welcome children into their beds), *nighttime is adult time.*

Introducing a grown child into your bed because 'she is scared when she comes home from her dad's' or some other such false justification annihilates your routine, decimates intimacy, and sets the stage for serious relationship dysfunction.

Because the Vampire has positioned you as a hero of lofty heights to her troubled daughter, any overtly 'fatherly' or authoritative act of sending the child to her own room will cause traumatic, shocking and devastating disappointment to the ten-year-old pawn in her game.

You cannot win this.

If you make the child go to her own room, you're a jerk. If you slip in a quip or a jab about how unhealthy and weird the situation is, then you are an insensitive meanie that doesn't have 'empathy' for how hard it is to be a single mom. If you calmly and assertively propose a strategy to help the child transition to her own bed, then you are 'trying to be her dad, and just don't like her watching movies with you at night-night time'.

If you say nothing, you will enjoy naught but a quick kiss and no sex. Because it is paralyzingly weird that there is some child the other side of your girlfriend, you will slowly and constantly scootch to the edge, subtly 'moving away from the craziness of it', and restlessly half-sleep on a sliver of the bed upon which you once sprawled out in free-form pleasure, relaxation and ecstasy, recalling in ongoing bouts of frustrating and vivid mental imagery how you but recently enveloped your lover in countless diverse types of snuggle formations.

If you get up and go sleep downstairs, you have become a roommate and no fiancé, boyfriend or husband.

YOU CANNOT WIN. That is the function and aim of the taboo.

Once you realize that your only chance of making love to your partner in your 'new normal' is sneaking in a quickie in the laundry room and that you will otherwise have no sex for a week, every other week – as your nighttime routine is now carved in half, you will lash out. You will protest, you will voice your worry about the erosion of the quality of your relationship; the lost nights, the fractured communication, the diminishing intimacy, the beginning of the ending of the optimal time for romance.

You will lash out, and you will lose.

Contrary to what 'the world' and Modernity proclaims – that 'children come first' – it is not so.

The tail does not wag the dog.

The head does not turn the neck.

The child does not rule the home.

For the Modern Knight, then, you cannot win this – but you can learn, once again, what *not* to do, if peradventure you get another chance at love.

- Your partner comes first
- Your partner comes first, and
- Your partner comes first

By actively, intentionally, and radically loving, revering, respecting, and honoring your woman – and modeling this with consistency – your children will have an example and course for becoming self-actualized adults, and not permanently entitled, coddled, arrested and juvenile future victims and sheep.

It is never appropriate for you to put your new partner in weird, awkward or bizarre situations where the children from a prior marriage or relationship are concerned.

It is never appropriate for you to make your partner think that they are part-time – a spouse when the kids are away and a roommate when they are with you.

The love ritual and end-of-day routine is one of the greatest gifts you can give your partner in a brutally difficult life. It is a safe time, a winding-down time, a sacred time, a time of romantic service, and a time to be naughty and fun. Do not defraud your future One and Only of this great gift!

CHAPTER 11
THE ADVANCED USE OF TABOOS AND DEEDS MADE TO ENSURE A CRAZY-MAKING RESPONSE
ACT 2
OF NEPHEWS AND HANDJOBS

The Psychic Femme Vampire comes from a small town.

The Psychic Femme Vampire hates the small town.

The Psychic Femme Vampire is self-loathing, for she IS small-town.

And for all the goodness, value and benefit of rural versus urban living, there are various dark things that sometimes occur in the farming communities, on the ranch or in the little oil town. For where virtue abounds, evil lurks. Where lack of activity and opportunity persists, idleness becomes the sandbox of the Devil. Sometimes family is *too close;* self-evident boundaries give way to perverse actual, potential or the appearances of shocking taboos.

This is her background, Aspen fashion or Scottsdale hair and make-up notwithstanding. And she will weaponize it...

Somewhere along the way, the Vampire fooled around with a cousin, made out with a foster-brother, or was inappropriate with an uncle. Or, perhaps, she taught her nephew some tricks to help him with the ladies during his 'developmental years'. Why wouldn't she? After all, she can:

- Use the most potent form of blackmail there is: *shame.* For who would believe that she seduced him? She can hear the prevailing thoughts in her satanic-super-computer mind. The townies proclaim that she is strikingly beautiful, immensely popular and overtly sweet. Surely the lad's hor mones overpowered his self-control and he initiated the untoward interludes, right? "She would not do such a thing; *she is too good for that, and frankly, doesn't belong here.*"

- Have a 'special bond'. Because boys love sex, the nephew may never, ever view himself as the victim of sexual abuse. Rather, he will venerate her as a goddess and, in his mind, an ally closer than any 'regular best friend'. He will have her back, because *he had her back,* for the rest of their lives, or until he tries to enter into a healthy, monogamous and adult relationship and finds he has severe issues – whichever comes first.

- Always have some known but not known, suspected yet never proven, leverage, tension or 'thing not to be uttered' between herself and her sister. For though the façade demands that she and her sister are besties, sisterhood is part of the nuclear family, and she hates her big sister too. That the nephew regards his aunt (the Vampire) above his own mother is a source of supply and smirking joy.

- Most importantly, possess and wield another depraved, crazy-making taboo as a weapon towards the men she will feast upon for the sum of her vampiric career.

Lastly, she may have simply witnessed her friends doing these things and never committed them herself. It will never be known and is not relevant whether she made out with her nephew or simply controls her kin through seduction, flirting and the manifestation of taboo sexual tension.

What is relevant is that this unmentionable taboo, like unto 'the Family Bed', will once again put her prospective Quiet Man into another woeful 'lose-lose' situation.

Its outworking may be as the following scenario:

You, the prospective Quiet Man, have been invited to a family meal back in the small town. The gathering includes her parents (her father a full corpse of a man; pale, too skinny, he speaks rarely, for when he does the scornful glare of his spouse follows in an instant, and he disappears back into his Scotch), her sister (who is simple, modest, beautiful and kind), and her adoptive sister (for her parents fostered as a self-aggrandizement before the local church), who is the family's one token homosexual. They disagree with who she is, what she does, and the aggressive, militant manner in which she imposes her views on the community. But they show their virtue by inviting her to Sunday late lunch/early dinner every week just the same. She skulks at the table and they patronize her via acquiescence to political correctness instead of simply relating to, challenging, debating, laughing with, encouraging and loving someone who happens to be different than the majority of those around her. You want to engage her, but do not.

Then there are cousins, significant others of cousins, the close neighbor fella who is 'like family', and lastly, her nieces and nephews.

The nephews' father is not at the family meal, for he (the Vampire's brother-in-law) is a chauvinistic narcissist (as are all men) and the family has finally convinced the Vampire's sister to try and leave him.

One nephew in particular is in his late teens. He is muscular, handsome and simple. In all the hustle and bustle of passing casseroles and family shouting over each other in between tiny bursts of short-lived 'listening' silences (for none are actively listening to one another – rather they are clamoring and posturing, waiting only to talk) the Quiet Man sees that this nephew sits oddly close to your girlfriend (his aunt). Nearly thigh to thigh with her at the table, he finds every occasion for horseplay, pinching and wrestling with her. All others act oblivious to this, as if it were taking place in a bubble or separate dimension, and their lack of acknowledgment enhances its awkwardness tenfold.

Your girlfriend, your soulmate, the woman with whom you make passionate love four times a week and twice on Saturdays (when her ten-year-old isn't home, invading your bed, that is...) – the very one who ever bemoans 'rednecks, inbreds and hillbillies' as despisable, lesser lifeforms – is not only not arresting his behavior, but is actually encouraging it with pokes and pinches of the lad's upper thigh or pelvis as adolescent new lovers do on long school bus rides in secondary school.

Then the nephew speaks, addressing her at the table.

In the place of the deep and virile voice of a young man whimpers the intentional sound of a three-year-old. A muscular oil rig worker or mechanic speaking as a squeaky, sniveling, grunting little piglet.

"Aaaaaaan-tie," he cries. "Aaaaaaannn-tie."

Not one of the twelve seated give any indication that the underdeveloped, crooning voice is untoward.

"Is it true you're not staying with us tonight?" he continues, protesting that his aunt (and your girlfriend) is sleeping with you and not he during the visit.

The Vampire slides closer, flinging the strong yet feminine embrace of her vines about him; cocooning him in strange family love; APOLOGIZING that she is not sleeping over, but consoling him that she will be sure to break away wherever possible over the long holiday weekend to spend one-on-one time with him.

He remains jealous but appeased by this, and the cartoon voice and salutation of "Aaaaan-tie" continues with every sentence.

In this situation, what can a gentleman and Knight do?

The instant that words of concern, no matter how gently and carefully forged, are mouthed, she will say that YOU are a sick freak for accusing her of incest. That her family is 'not like that', that he 'has simply had a rough life at the hands of his narcissistic father' and that only a cold, insensitive and perverse bastard would think it anything less than what it so innocently was.

Of course, the nephew is later and often recurringly heard telling friends that he wants to beat you up for stealing his "Aaaaan-tie" from him – but I digress. YOU are the perverse one, not she.

This technique, where the one who cries "The barn is on fire!" is immediately branded the arsonist, is as old as Fallen Man. She has simply perfected the tactic, adding taboo sexual inappropriateness to a tried and true game. If you respond, it is good for at least a dozen scrumptious fights to her – a feast of your essence as a person.

If you say nothing and carry on with no acknowledgment of her 'close family relationship' with the young nephew, even better. The lack of acknowledgment of the weird or the shocking creates a weird, subservient and traumatized silence or 'make-believe' in your ensuing day-to-day actions. She will guzzle down the negative energy of that quiet defeat as a thirsty child slams a slushie on a hot summer day after playing football for two hours.

And moreover, if she can do that with neither response (save the defeated nothingness, which *is a response*), then she can do the next thing, and the next...

CHAPTER 12
THE ADVANCED USE OF TABOOS AND DEEDS MADE TO ENSURE A CRAZY-MAKING RESPONSE
ACT 3
ACTUALLY, NOT EVERYBODY POOPS

Most men are lewd and rude.

Most women are not. And they neither favor nor enjoy lewdness.

A couple's policy for belching, flatulence, visiting the washroom with the door open in an attention-gathering 'look at me' manner, for constant discussions of, musings about, or actually imposing 'fluids, gasses and vulgar acts' on one another should be discussed and well-known very early in the relationship. That a woman is a special vessel created by God to be revered, honored and doted upon, and *not* farted on under the bedsheets, is another controversial truth that was so self-evident as to not need explanation, clarification, or even mention just a generation ago. But alas, here we are, having to touch upon unmentionables in the post-truth dispensation.

Of the endless sea of harm feminism has visited upon women, the license for men to be disgusting pigs in their presence may be paramount; for, after all, "there is no difference between boys and girls."

But there is.

It is offputting, contrary to nature and TABOO when a man imposes acts, words or deeds that belong in the restroom upon or near his girlfriend or spouse. More so, it is QUADRUPLE TABOO when SHE does these things in kind of her own accord!

The Psychic Vampire knows this truth, and she knows that you know it as well. Therefore, seeking a gentleman who will be put off, shocked, disgusted, confused and unbalanced when she transforms overnight from debutante to troll is amongst her favorite hunting strategies.

There are noted exceptions where eccentric or unique couples enjoy belching and other rude ruminations; these are the famous, or comedically and adorably infamous, marvels of their friends and loved ones. In these cases, the individuals were fully transparent about their proclivities and ways from the beginning, and the 'potty humor' was part of their journey, not a rapid and random departure from it. Consistency is the hallmark of health; random and purposeful behavior changes the markers of ill motives.

But for the remainder of those who choose to love and love actively, whether at age twenty-three or seventy-nine, there will be no barging in whilst she is visiting the washroom, making intentionally disgusting noises in her presence, or treating her as if she is 'one of the guys in the locker room'. Respect does not change with the season; reverence doth not fade with comfort.

The indicators for this taboo may play out as follows:

At the onset of the relationship, the Vampire acknowledges that there is something different about you (and this feels very good). That you are a 'throwback to a more golden age', knightly and polite. She will go out of her way to let you know that she sees you are a gentleman and not at all like the other foul men in her life who are ever making poop jokes or classifying, ranking and celebrating their bowel movements.

She will call out in the most positive light your deep respect for her, and she will use humor to confirm with you that she shares your beliefs and approach in this regard, saying, "As you know, my love, woman actually do not even go 'number two'."

After the establishment of views and shared compliments over the undesirable topic, it is retired to the closet (where it belongs) and is simply not needed to be mentioned again. You revere and honor her and are not a disgusting pig. It's noted; onward you move into living life and cultivating your partnership.

Then, three months later... a change.

It was never a possibility in your mind, or even a fly-speck-sized dot on your radar, that SHE would be the repulsive one.

It starts randomly one day. She suddenly starts sharing, in micro-detail, her 'gastro' medical history and problems. Noting that these problems weren't present in the last 104 nights you've spent with her, you are interested and concerned, but perplexed.

All at once, she is obsessed – with poop.

She has a gleam in her eye when discussing the topic; a half-tilted smirk that says 'I know this makes you uncomfortable, and thus I will redouble the quantity and intensity so that you ARE UNCOMFORTABLE, and stimulated to respond.' For it is ever about the response.

The princess that once smelled ever as rose petals garnished with vanilla, or when being seductive, gave airs of seductive musks and sultry scents, is now winds of sulfur, clouds of giggly, toxic fogs of 'toots and bubbles'.

Suddenly, randomly, dozens of times per day she bids you not to stand down-wind of her; she chews her gum as if she is angry with it, and masticates her food as a woodland ogre instead of the lady you came to romantically worship. From princess to piglet in three to four months.

When the change in this category is upon the prey, he may be compelled to:

- Laugh
- Join in the lifestyle change

Do neither of these things!

Again, she has borrowed a page from the playbook of what abusive men do to their partners. It is an old, old (and cruel) game, and she has appropriated it. Typically, men are gentlemen early in a relationship for the purpose of 'hooking and reeling in' a lass

– only then to become fat, lazy and gross once they've won her. It's called a 'bait and switch', and it results in a woman bemoaning "Where is the man I married?!"

When a man is vulgar in the presence of his lady, it means the following:

- He does not respect her
- He believes he 'owns her'
- He has neither care nor worry for continuing to woo her, pursue and win her affections, or keep her
- He is comfortable with or without her. She is just 'part of the furniture in the apartment now'

It is at once a form of unhealthy control and the devaluation of his mate when a man does it.

The Vampire knows this, for she learned it from her mentor, who is an expert at studying what men do when they are mistreating women – and how to both invert and improve upon the tactics.

It will never be known what is real, what is a show, or what is unleashed simply to produce the crazy-making response. She may be shy and modest in earnest (consistent with the early days of the courtship) and simply goading the Quiet Man in hopes that he feeds her with his shock and protests. Conversely, she may be the ogre who was but disguised as a princess for a time. This is irrelevant, for love is consistent, transparent and honest.

As with The Family Bed and The Close-Close Nephew, this taboo is designed to create another lose-lose scenario for the Modern Knight. The instant that the man protests or opposes her behavior, he will be forever and irrevocably branded as:

- Insensitive. What kind of selfish monster won't listen to and be supportive of her health problems?
- Controlling. Who is he to tell her what she can and cannot talk about?
- Domineering. Why can't she just be comfortable in her own skin? After all, it's not the honeymoon period anymore.

- Feminine. Here the Vampire, although a champion of third-wave, militant feminism, will behind the scenes and apart from the public call the man 'feminine', 'squeamish' or even a 'faggot' for not reveling in her farts.

Contrariwise, the instant the man endorses her behavior, joining in the new era of belching contests, ass-picking and lip-smacking, he is at once and forever:

- A disrespectful jerk. If she does it it's cute – after all, she's a lady.
- A trickster. He will be the one accused of the 'bait and switch'.
- Lastly, and worst of all, neither of the above. Rather, she will allow, empower and encourage it, giving unspoken and smirking endorsement that the gilded and lofty, romantic, Shakespearean-level love you thought you shared is no more, or never was. The vibe, nature, look and feel of the partnership has changed forever, and for the worse.

What can be done? Remember, Modern-Day Knight, you are responsible for your response, always and in all ways.

1. Never answer lewdness with lewdness. Be polite, be mindful, be sensitive, and do not get hooked by the ankle only to be dragged downward into the gutter.

2. There is an artful way to participate in the humor at a light level with one or, at the most, two reciprocations of the banter. And no more. Use good leadership skills to shift the conversation away to the nine million other things in the human experience that could serve as a medium for humor or fun discourse.

3. Call her bluff. If she truly has medical issues, then act to resolve them. Book her a doctor's appointment, buy her probiotics, *act* to find a root cause and serve your partner. (Those who do struggle with IBS, Crones or other gastro challenges are the very last people on God's green

earth to make constant jokes and raunchy comments about it. The vamp has appropriated their real issues unto herself because it is in vogue to be afflicted, and hip for women to act in accord with the lesser angels of masculinity as a declaratory ensign of feminism).

Do not sacrifice your soul or your vision for what a mutually respectful and loving partnership should be, Modern-Day Knight, on the altar of 'being one of the guys with your girlfriend'.

Never, ever, ever, under any circumstance, use the washroom with the door open...

CHAPTER 13
THE BROKEN HEARTS SHIT-TALKER CLUB

The aforementioned taboos and plethora of other like engineered lose-lose scenarios are exhausting. Contrary to the mainstream formula for dealing with a narcissistic partner, this book does not reactively and readily cry out "Leave him/her!" or "No-contact policy!". Such notions presuppose that the Vampire (or Werewolf) are victims of their own environment, are not accountable, not capable of change.

They are *not* victims (though they are often broken-hearted and misguided by the jaded, the political and academic elite, and/or the equally broken-hearted), they *own* their choices, and they *can* change.

None of that makes the grind and gruel of sojourning through a swamp of strange taboo and gross unmentionables any easier to suffer, especially after the euphoric height of your galactic, honorable, wondrous fairy-tale beginnings. The Psychic Vampire is cunning and highly intelligent. And she knows you are now:

- Bewildered
- Tired
- On edge

These are morsels for her. Appetizers.

To 'fatten you up' and render you plump, juicy and ready to be consumed as a main course, she will feign flattery and 'rebuild you'. Slinging over-the-top criticisms and slander about her ex in intense 'sessions' with her girlfriends, family or associates in your presence is amongst her favorite methods for seeing you lifted up ere your next scheduled fall.

In fact, such obsessive, critical, man-hating rants were probably present from the beginning – only the Quiet Man candidate, being smitten, did not notice them. After all, it feels good, initially, to be set out and contrasted from her past partners in verbal celebrations with her friends and family as 'The One', 'The Only Nice Guy Left Alive', 'Finally, A Man Who Gets It', the '5D Self-Actualized Demigod' or other glowing designations of the same kind.

These sessions are frequent, relentless, loud, vulgar and 'over the top'. The Quiet Man candidate, and other Quiet Men, if the other women have allowed their collection of supply to be present (remember, this is a cult: she is not alone, and neither are you), sit there sedate and submissive at the table or upon the couch, drinking their beer or coffee with head down and opinions concealed; confining their discourse to the weather, hunting or sports. Meanwhile, the Vampire (remember, the one who professes herself an introvert) looses screeching invective that originates from nowhere about how her ex:

- Never paid the bills
- Is a horrible parent
- Cheated on her endlessly
- Berated her
- Criticized her about everything
- Couldn't function sexually anyhow
- Is now once again dating a twenty-three-year-old
- Is stupid
- Doesn't understand women
- Is neanderthal
- Hit her
- Dragged her about by the hair
- Is – a – narcissist

And the rant festivals are not delivered in precept or principle only. Rather, she and her venom-circle spare no detail in sharing story after story after story of the exact time, place, season and day of the week in which they were wronged. The discomfort of it is heavy, made worse as she throws you the crumb of contrasting compliments about how *you* would never do this, or that.

If you attend five family outings, the high-anger, shrill male-bashing has occurred five times.

If you have gone out for drinks with her and three of her friends six times in three months, then you have witnessed wine- or hard-seltzer-accompanied hate-filled slanderous rants about past lovers – six times.

It is absolute and unrelenting. She simply cannot, and will not, cease from talking about him. *She brings him to every meal. There is not a single day during which he is not referenced.*

And now, several months on, the yo-yo of inconsistency, the vanishing affection, and the ever-present weight of nightly gross, untoward or peculiar taboos begets one powerful by-product:

Perspective. Objective Perspective.

Where once you sat round the table quietly as she and her sister, aunt or neighbor droned on and on about how bad he was and how good you are, believing that indeed he was 'that bad' and you 'that good' (the truth being that the ex was not 'that bad', neither are you 'that good'), basking in the compliments, blushing at how much the group of ladies like you – now there is careful, logical evaluation.

The fog lifting, the Quiet Man candidate now sits at the same table and realizes:

1. That a current girlfriend or wife who speaks of her former spouse or partner in such quantity is not a compliment to you. It is assuredly the opposite. Negative comments in high volumes are obsessive, bringing to light the fact that *he* is ever-present in her thoughts. And the same is true for her circle, who cannot stop speaking about their exes.

2. The group of women is actually feasting on negativity and the putting down of men. Benign conversations about bills, movies or mundane topics of fancy always, always veer right

back into a rant about 'past men', whether relevant or not.

As the flattery of being complimenting (at his expense) has worn off, you are able to periscope back and remove self from the equation. Upon doing this, empathy for this individual wells within you:

- He's not here to defend himself.
- There are multiple perspectives to every story.
- It is wrong to insult ANY person behind their back.

Awareness brings understanding, and the Quiet Man comes to understand the following:

- These women are each of them obsessed with their exes, and likely still in love with them. For the old adage regarding the thin line between love and hate now empirically seems quite true.
- They are feasting on each other's negativity. It's a drug, and they cannot stop themselves.
- Every man is evil in their eyes – and guess what? That you are the Golden Boy and Chosen One they adore is an utter illusion and lie.

Now you realize that a few months or a few years from now, a new Quiet Man will be sitting where you are right now – and YOU will simply be the subject of their shit-talking at the very same table!

There are deep lessons to be gleaned here that will help both new couples (especially young men) and those who have struggled with break-ups and are re-entering the dating scene in/after their mid-thirties.

For the Modern-Day Knight, heed these well and make them part of your practice and approach at all times:

1. **Your partner is a goddess and rockstar, and your compliments of her stand on their own merits.** There are over six billion great things about her, and they don't need to be compared to anyone or anything. It's not a market, she's not a piece of fruit; she's a person (and your person), and you are accountable for ensuring she feels edified and lifted

up and never caused to think of you with another.

2. **Ensure 'compare and contrast' is minimal.** There is a temptation to compliment her via comparison. It will happen, but make a deliberate effort to make such statements infrequently, or not at all. Elsewise she will just wonder (fairly) why you are even thinking about past lovers, ranking, contrasting, etc. It is perfectly fine to declare her "the best kisser of all time!" without the follow-up of "Rebecca was a horrible kisser."

3. **Have a policy of respect and neighborly love towards your ex, no matter what.** Your attitude as a gentleman and knight ought to be one of neighborly love garnished with neutrality, and no more. You are not hung up on your ex enough to give her place in your heart (or to carry her luggage into your new relationship), to cause bitterness, malice or invective. Your new partner will appreciate that you have no vested interest, either negative nor positive, and will be impressed that you are honorable towards all women. In this regard, she will trust that, should you unfortunately ever break up or part ways, your intimate conversations, shortcomings and dirty laundry won't be angrily shared when you are 'with the fellas'. Women value integrity. Be a man of intentional integrity and honor.

4. **Guard against speaking ill of anyone, and doubly so when carried away in a group setting.** There is nothing more dangerous in politics, business or matters of the heart than 'the mob'. Otherwise kind people engage in overt cruelty when the passions of the crowd whip them up, and thoughtful individuals become downright rude when the energy of the impassioned masses compel them.

Be aware of our fallen condition and tendency to slander, ridicule, 'talk shit' and act untowardly when 'in the group'; carry a filter and monitor... and knock it off.

CHAPTER 11
WE DON'T WANT TO HEAR
ABOUT OTHER MEN'S PENISES

The Psychic Femme Vampire's use of 'comparison technique' is not limited to her hateful, vicious (and pterodactyl-level-loud) rant fests with her girlfriends. She does it when she and her partner are alone too.

As with the more public iteration, this is often present early in the courtship, but simply missed during the euphoria of falling in love with her. Even in the very first lovemaking encounter, subtle seeds that she is ever thinking about other men may be present:

- "My ex was never this hard."
- "He couldn't keep it up."
- "We couldn't even have sex towards the end. Well, not intercourse anyhow."
- "I love how you take command – he never knew what to do."
- "You're the only one that makes me orgasm more than once."

These are woven and blended with an artful tapestry of actual and legitimate compliments, playful humor during and after love-making, steamy seduction, and fantastic sex.

But as her skilled use of taboo, intentional erraticism, 'hot-cold' behavior, and the chronic lies she tells her children and her friends compounds and escalates, the mind of the Quiet Man is able to recollect, hindsight revealing seeds of promiscuity and control from the beginning.

The real reasons she continues to make reference to other men include:

1. Broken heart: the Vampire, like her literary counterpart, is permanently and perpetually dead and undead, stuck going through the motions of the mortals, cursed with a deeply broken heart. Any excuse to lash out, hurt or destroy you gives her opportunity to reminisce about the one who spurned her.

2. The green taboo: if you render a response over her endless past penis performances, YOU will be the bad guy – the jealous, controlling, narcissistic jerk.

3. Promiscuity and perversion: she is flaunting the fact, most overtly, that she collects penises. A steady stream of endless contrasting references (bigger, better skilled, longer lasting, better oral pleasures, etc.), under the pretext of compli menting you actually does the opposite. She is telling you that you are being ranked, categorized and added to the scorecard in her mind; and that you will be part of her benchmarking data for use with her next lover.

4. Hatred of men: remember, **the Psychic Vampire loves dick but hates men, vehemently.** All men are evil, and the only thing of value they provide is the short-lived pleasure from the member between their legs.

Just as men struggle to actively and intentionally learn how women think, feel and function in the world, many women fail to understand how men think, feel and function in this world.

Here, then, is the undiluted truth of how we prefer the matter of 'past lovers' to be managed. I make no value judgement on whether it be right or wrong, rational or irrational, good or bad. However, if a woman seeks insight into how her partner operates – here it is.

We do not want to think about another man inside the woman we love. Ever. Regardless of whether it was ten years or three months ago: Not Ever. Whether it was her most recent relationship or four relationships ago: Never. Under no circumstance, ever, do we desire to put our thoughts, emotions or mind's eye in that traumatic scenario.

We prefer the delightful delusion that she is a virgin when we meet, though she be twenty and four, thirty-seven or three score and seven. And that we are her 'first and last'.

Behind the pseudo-veneer of machismo, men are soft, romantic beings who want to be her one and only, and we absolutely want to feel and believe that she in kind is our one and only. We live in a fallen and flawed world and, of course, realize that the reality of this standing is unrealistic. Thus, it is not a matter of shame or imputing guilt, hypocritical judgement or even, as often occurs, anger against a woman for her past (or our past) – but we don't want it thrust in our face either.

Moreover, men do not, in reality, compare, their juvenile locker-room boasts notwithstanding. It simply doth not occur. In the same regard that there is a God-given erasing of each phase of parenting (just ask the parent of a teenager if they *really* recall what toddlers were like. They will tell you that it was the most wondrous and easy time of their life, to the raucous laughter of parents actually toiling through that chapter. God causes us to forget each chapter so that we can yearn for it anew, make more babies, and perpetuate ourselves), so too are past lovers forgotten so that men can seek a new lover as though she were truly new, and love again.

We are not thinking of 'her' breasts, privy or hinder parts when making love to our new (and hopefully 'forever') partner. And when holding hands or kissing (which are paramount, where intimacy is concerned, above intercourse), we are utterly, wholly and exclusively in the present with our new lady-loves.

Any honest man will testify the same.

It is only when single or alone that the lust of a past haunt (or joy) that can never quite fully be reconstructed in the mind, the heart or the loins renews within a man.

Men are so myopic in the laser focus of the task, relationship, quest or battle at hand that we ponder little else. For this cause, the idea that she is contemplating, comparing, ranking and openly discussing 'other penises' is a deeply injurious offense to men.

CHAPTER 15
SPEAKING OF PENISES: THE VAMPIRE CULT HAS NO OBJECTION TO SHARING THEM WHEN HER BEST FRIEND IS HER EX'S EX

The Psychic Femme Vampire is not a solitary practitioner of her craft. Although she ultimately (and behind the scenes) envies, hates, slanders, defames, and devalues those in her coven (she does this in the Quiet Man's presence, for what can he say against her?), they publicly work together and in concert to encourage each other's misery and the destruction of their common enemy (men, women, the nuclear family, etc.).

She possesses zero qualms about discussing past sex partners, in detail, with great frequency, with either her current lover (the prey) or her circle of friends. Equally, she has no sense of 'conflict of interest' with respect to making 'best friends' of her exes' current or former girlfriends/spouses.

Whilst she denounces her ex as the devil himself, as the King of all Narcissists, she cleaves to his new girlfriend, who in turn is portrayed as the most hoodwinked, wounded, naïve and abused woman to ever live. After all, she is dating the *Monster of all Monsters,* despite her dear friend's wise and dire and daily counsel. And more than this, they are not just casual acquaintances: the covert narc has made a BEST FRIEND of her ex's girlfriend/spouse!

This means that, in addition to an ongoing supply of feeding off the negative energy syphoned from meddling and solicited daily reports of drama, degradation and abuse from the same source that used to feed the Vampire directly for so many months or even years (a sort of twisted second-hand psychic appetizer platter), she also gets the added bonus of staying intimately involved in the happenings of her ex's life (after all, she *is* still in love with him). In this regard, she gets to remain his wife or partner via proxy; and this is exhilarating to her.

That his One True Love noodles around with her ex's girlfriend is weird, off-putting and even inappropriate to the Quiet Man from the beginning. However, the Vampire quickly counters with two defensible excuses:

1. If she has a child, the justification narrative is simple. For the continuity of collaborative co-parenting, it behooves the Vampire to be friendly to the ex's new girlfriend. However, the outworking of this relationship is not merely strategic or neighborly. It is intimate and wholly separate from or focused on the child, who is often just a prop in the scheme. This excuse is a pretext, a lie.

2. The Mentor. The Vampire is a martyr and must sacrificially protect the poor misguided and seduced soul that is her ex's new girlfriend. Elsewise how will the poor lass survive? This positions the Vampire in the role of the empath, helping others regardless of how inappropriate it looks to the world, or to her new mate.

This circles The Quiet Man right back into the 'lose-lose' scenario zone. If he protests that her being best friends with her ex's partner is off-putting and bizarre then he is a controlling, insecure jerk. Who is he to say who her friends should be? If he lumps it, suffering the situation, then he is weak; silently drooping with a shoulder-forward slouch on the couch as she and the best friend talk about the military hero turned abuser over and over and over and over and over again, literally in every conversation. (Ironically, the Quiet Man never actually meets the Vampire's ex. There is never a 'man-to-man' handshake, beer or cup of coffee.

To his credit, the Monster at least has the basic common sense to avoid such a peculiar and unhealthy threesome, not wanting to ever make it a quartet. *For men don't share vaginas the way some women share penises.)* The Femme Vamp notes this weakness and increases the taboo by degree, progressively. She cheats on him repeatedly, rewarding his sensitivity and open-mindedness with punitive and chronic betrayal.

- If open and honest, then he is defamed as a controlling chauvinist; lose.
- If submissive and acquiescent, then he is steamrolled as a doormat; lose.

And the friendship is not one of equal footing. They are not peers. The Vampire mentors her proxy. The proxy girlfriend is invariably a younger version of the Vampire and, through the process of influence and time, assumes the fashion, make-up and hairstyle, vernacular and even romantic routines of her forebearer.

This creates a readymade mocking opportunity for the Vampire. When cuddling and making pillow-talk with the Quiet Man, she slanderously slams the Monster for not being able to get over their relationship, instead finding a 'younger version of her' to keep his bed warm. In reality, the Vampire 'made the replacement' as an excuse for more occasion and conjured cause to remain connected to her lost love.

The only thing favored above living through an extended version of the relationship with her ex through her protégé-clone is, ironically, causing and presiding over a break-up, and then feasting upon the break-up trauma. The Vampire carefully calculates what will yield her more negative energy, performing a sadistic cost-to-benefit analysis. To feast upon daily quips and squawks about how bad he is, and be near him that way, or to be the shadowy shoulder to cry upon, and be well drunken on the elixir of a traumatic break-up that forges a powerful Exes' Club? This is the question!

Both supply her in different ways, but the formation of *two* abused former partners, 'Narcissistic-Abuse-Survivor Sisters', is simply too scrumptious to pass up! Thus the Mentor advises the Protégé to discard, devalue and dump the Narcissist.

The pretend introvert finds the energy of ten thousand suns as she screams about the Monster and his real or pretended offenses against her best friend. The volume of yelling on the phone about what he did and how he did the same thing to her in their relationship vibrates the walls upstairs and the Quiet Man, down in the living room, sinks further and further into the television – and a Scotch – as the hours once given to deep conversation, playful wit, and gooey complements are now devoted to a cyclone of negativity that, as the Vampire and her friend re-live the fighting, discard and recovery plans, flood the home, suffocating all life therein.

For Modern-Day Knights: do not enter into relationships that are a conflict of interest, perceived or actual. It is not appropriate for you to be gladhanding with someone who used to sleep with your partner, or with one of your former partners. This is a chain of trouble best avoided through distance and boundaries.

Once the Vampire latched upon her protégé, the young lady's relationship was doomed to fail. The Vampire sowed seeds of discord, which were inevitably taken home to 'the Monster', causing him to have to deal with the woman he left five years ago afresh every few days!

As the Quiet Man watches this unfold and feels his light diminish, he ought to focus not on the loss of attention, respect, and romance, but rather on what is coming next. For what might happen if the Vampire opens recruitment and seeks a new friend for expansion of the coven? Did not the Quiet Man once have a past relationship with another woman from their small town? What might happen if they align to ignite their introverted empathetic rage towards... *him?*

CHAPTER 15
EVERY EX WAS A NARC — OR WERE THEY?

The Covert Narcissist is an avid reader/listener of every psychology journal, online video, social media group or podcast pertinent to their favorite subject: narcissistic personality disorder. In their worldview, Man is a product of his environment and is fated to think, feel and behave as he does due to external forces, which may include:

- Parental relationship (for male narcissists, a keen focus is made on their 'mommy issues')
- Socioeconomic circumstances
- Childhood trauma
- Culture
- Religious upbringing
- Race
- Penis/vagina
- Other

The Narcissist is drawn to this manner of thinking (though they know in their heart that it's bollocks, as do the Elites that peddle such folly) as it is a systematic theology, a Religion of Excuses. A formal and academically approved justification package for letting them off the hook.

There is no such thing as an individual in the mind of the Modernists or Post-Modernists (the fount that produces notions such as 'Personality Type' and 'Personality Disorder'), and absolutely no place for personal accountability, free will, or choice. Only the section or cross-section is paramount; only the victimization and outrage of the group possesses meaning.

It is currently popular to subdivide the whole of humanity into two major sub-groups (and then continue to sub-divide, segment and group them from there). Those who are not diagnosed with narcissistic personality disorder (fortunately for them, there is a diagnosis for literally *everything*) are:

- Designated as victims
- Sectionalized
- Managed and controlled based upon their groups/ designations
- Governed by Personality Type and the perceived attributes/ stereotypes of their group(s) and section(s)

Those diagnosed with, identified as, or branded as having a narcissistic personality disorder are:

Designated as villains

- Paradoxically held to strict standards of personal account-ability whilst simultaneously declared to be incapable of change or cure
- Governed by Personality Type and group designation

Narcissism is the only Personality Disorder that is vilified, lacking a celebratory month or parade, and not ogled by those obsessed with identity politics. There are no patches, flags, banners or logos for Narc-Personality-Disorder-identified beings.

This begs the query: why? If the narcissist is a victim of his or her environment, mommy, self-esteem deficiency, childhood abuse or other external force, why is he or she branded a monster only fit for tarring and feathering?

There is an obvious, glaring, beaming answer for those with eyes to see. And one only need look to the childhood playground or their favorite espionage film for the key.

Doth not the REAL VILLAIN ever create false villains to distract from his wicked, scheming deeds? Is not the Devil's most successful method, making of everyone else a devil whilst his existence is in the shadows, oft not even acknowledged to exist?

Let the reader's memory travel back to grade school and recall the two types of bullies, which exactly and precisely match the two narcissistic archetypes:

- **The Werewolf Bully.** He was openly a monster, terrorizing other kids through bombastic sarcasm, aggressive energy and, sometimes, physical strength. You knew this bully was coming. He was awful. He would get the entire playground laughing at your braces, then punch you in the stomach and steal your lunch money. But he was 'the devil you knew', and you could prepare for him accordingly.

- **The Vampire Bully.** He was quiet, brooding, reserved and intellectual. His mode of power and destruction was to pin his crimes on the 'other kid', to make everyone a bully save himself, and to control the playground through drama, intrigue, and manipulation. Ever the ruminating victim, this bully was 'the devil in disguise', hard to anticipate, hard to counter. He would steal your lunch money from your locker and then sulk in the classroom quietly and influence events just so that the teacher pinned the crime on the werewolf, or on you.

The Werewolf Bully peaked in high school and was likely humbled in college or during his early twenties. Finding out ultimately that he was not the strongest, tallest or best at this or that, he adjusted his approach, found reasonableness and ceased selfishly being the destructive 'look at me' center of the universe. Moreover, he often comes to realize that steamrolling individuals, colleagues, family or spouses is both abusive and wholly ineffective. Usually, the Werewolf Bully repents and matures. When he does not, he becomes the lifelong openly mean jerk, easy to mark and avoid.

The Vampire Bully may grow up to be a psychologist, academic or thought leader (where he seeks to find acolytes to mentor or influence), but more frequently enters a successful but unassuming 'back-office' trade where he can mock exceptionalism, put down creativity, and scheme in the shadows. His covert control continues throughout life. All others are bullies; he alone is good, enlightened and in tune.

Thus, when your spouse or girlfriend uses the term 'narcissist' for every man she's ever dated, and even every person with whom she disagrees; when all men are inherently abusive, born as controlling, unevolved Neanderthals; when every girlfriend is a 'selfish bitch' and every family member 'crazy and mean'; when constant is the categorizing of others and the judgement of all as sick, all as broken, all as toxic; when all these are non-stop, and combined with taboos and heaping lies, you are dating a Covert Narcissist – a Vampire who brands others with all the things that she is.

And here is where it pains me to advise men primarily in their thirties, seeking a second or third chance at love, that they must sacrifice a little romance for a lot of peace.

Although they want life to be a living sweet sonnet, a field of daffodils with faeries dancing and sprites crooning melodic hymns of all-conquering love (and it is right and good to want these things), the reality is more like social media research and a few interviews... and maybe a background check.

When the accusations of her ex being a psychopathic monster and abusive narcissist are laid upon you thrice daily:

- DO NOT let the putting him down make YOU feel good. This is a trap
- DO ask the question within: *Is he, though?*
- DO research

You may find startling and hard truths.

For example, although she claims her ex-husband (the war hero) beat her mercilessly, cut her, concussed and hospitalized her often, that the abuse caused physical and emotional scars from which she may never recover, you may find a preponderance of evidence that this is not so.

- He 'beat her about the face with closed fists', yet her father still goes fishing with him. The divorce was six years ago, yet they are taking photos holding the 'big one' together... two weeks ago.

- He 'dragged her from the shower when pregnant'. The ruptures, bruising and trauma resulting in her losing the baby, yet her own mother thanks him for his service, 'likes' every post, and publicly calls him a 'good father, a good man'.

Let common sense prevail. As a parent of a beautiful, brilliant, powerful and vibrant daughter (as is this writer), consider how you would think, feel and operate were any man to harm the slightest hair upon her head, let alone abuse and torture your daughter. Fathers revere, love, adore, provide for and sacrifice all to see their girls safe, happy and strong.

Peradventure you may (and peradventure equally may not), through God's grace and leaning upon His supernatural succor of strength to forgive, find some ability to not end up in jail for slaying the bastard and drinking his blood. You may even get to the place where you can be in the same zip code as he without firebombing his car.

One thing is certain, however: you will never go fishing with the scum that did THAT to your girl.

Indeed. This is because the ex in question is NOT the scum she portrays, and YOU will be the next one she portrays as doing monstrous things when the time has come for her to discard you and feed upon the next one.

This is not to move to the other side of the ledger and knight the fellow or make of him an angel. Indeed, he may well have been a jerk. But branding a jerk as a narcissist devalues real villainy, and creates a 'here we go again' collective societal fatigue that ends up **not giving the due support, focus and singular energy needed to help women who are ACTUALLY being abused.**

The Psychic Vampire's favorite name to call her exes is narcissist, because she is a narcissist.

The Psychic Vampire will call you the same if you protest her taboos, erraticism, hot-cold technique, or the craters left by her love bombs. You can be a narcissist or a Quiet Man; a villain or a victim.

This is the false dichotomy she seeks to place you in and the one you must endeavor to avoid. *For you are neither of these.*

Again, it is not recommended that a couple in their youth research, poke around in, or in any sense use and weaponize the past as he or she builds the future with their new (and hopefully first and only) partner. In that wonderful situation (O, how youth is wasted on the young!), they are EACH OTHER'S reference checks, each other's past.

It is a painful truth, unfortunately, that the same cannot be said for those on round two or three of seeking a lasting relationship in a fallen world.

CHAPTER 17
MORE ON CHEATING...

In the same regard that the Vampire concludes every man to be a narcissist because *she is a narcissist,* she also views all men as cheaters, applying Old-Testament-intensity rules and restrictions on her partner whilst she is humping the whole neighborhood.

She is a chronic cheater.

She is a serial cheater.

A fair question might be "Why?" or "How did she come to be this way?" Of a truth, there is no real 'why', exemption or justification for betrayal. Just ask the person cheated on – they will not wax philosophic about daddy issues and upbringings.

The blunt 'why' is that she chooses, with her own free will, to cheat. She does not, at least during the moment or season of infidelity, love you enough to choose to be faithful.

These reductions are not meant to simplify a complex, fallen world. There are stimuli, situations and scenarios that *tempt* a man or woman to cheat – but at the end of the day, they choose who they kiss, to whom they text late-night and early morning love missives, to whom they give their bodies and affections.

In the case of the Psychic Vampire, the motive remains constant.

- She grew up in a small town that she loathed
- She escaped into military or professional circles
- She met a boy
- Her love was unrequited

At that moment she opted to take the course of a monster and inflict her scorn on all future lovers, feeding the abyss of her pain with the energy, strife, drama and submission of men who actually love her and innocently have no part in what made her this way. As a result, she begets broken-hearted men who in turn may choose to become as she.

Unrequited love. A cruel force unmatched for pain in the cosmos. Where those with a naturalist, atheistic or other non-Christian worldview would explain these behaviors via the mind, this writer would proclaim it to be a matter of the heart.

Love cures everything. Love conquers all. By inversion, unrequited or misplaced love destroys everything, and defeats all.

These are the inconsistences you can and should expect once fanged by the femme fatale and finding yourself a Quiet Man in embryo:

- The Green Taboo reminder – she will have questionable relationships with other men, be they work colleagues, high-school friends, 'the gay friend that is more like her girlfriend', the 'lewd guy who has no shot with her but she keeps him around', and other varieties of collections of men that just 'feel off' or inappropriate to any reasonable gentleman.

- However, outside of minimal viable and necessary contact for work, you must have no contact with any humanoid that happens to have a vagina. If you do, you are a cheater.

- Wished a colleague from work 'Merry Christmas' on social media? Cheater.

- Said something complimentary, full of class, and utterly benign about a female leader or business owner? Definitely cheating.

- She will be yucking it up with the male neighbor who shows up every day when you are not there and tries to take out your trash and 'help' her. Not cheating.

- Laughing and cackling over dick pics with her military friends? Not cheating.

- Having male overnight house guests when you are away on business? Not cheating.

- Having dinner with an ex-boyfriend just to make you uncomfortable one hour before a presentation? Not cheating.
- But you, sir, shall look at no other, talk to no other, interact with no other for so long as you live in her prison of inconsistency, betrayal and hypocrisy!

But this chapter – nay, this book – is not about her. It is about the Modern-Day Knight. It is about you. The Quiet Man entangled in this scenario must learn and accept the lesson of how not to treat his partner and how to be a better, more consistent person and leader.

As with the greater portion of this treatise, men happen to be much, much worse about hypocrisy in the 'cheating or questionable behavior' zone. It is usually men who follow, act out and personify every bullet above. By contrast, women are generally very loyal and seldom cheat. The Psychic Vampire seems to have borrowed from what abusive men do, then perfected the craft.

The Modern-Day Knight should not walk around thinking that this will happen again and again in future relationships. He should focus on his own conduct and not worry about external forces or people who ultimately own their own choices. The gentleman should actually hold *himself* to some of the standards that she is imposing on him – but rooted in love, morality, empathy and commitment, not stressful, nasty, hypocritical orders.

For this cause:

- A man in a marriage or committed, serious relationship should not be friends with women. This may rank as another *revolutionary, yet obvious, yet somehow controversial truth.* Although some women can, on occasion, have male friends, the reverse is not true. A man never, ever, ever wants to 'just be friends'; the notion is dishonest to the core and ever leads to destruction and despair, ranging from awkward lifelong 'friendzone' dynamics to outright affairs and every permeation of heartache and heartbreak in between. Man is created to bed down and mate the Woman. This is the design, regardless of how much modernity may wish to deny, redefine, or ignore it.

- This in no way suggests that men should not be friendly, neighborly, and kind to all people, regardless of gender. However, a man in a committed relationship should not enter into *close relationships* with members of the opposite sex.

- A man should not ogle other women. Keep your eyes, your lustful thoughts and your comments to your own woman. She is a treasure, a glorious vessel, and you are beyond blessed that she even talks to you.

- Avoid situations that give the appearance of impropriety. Perception can become as truth, and situations that 'look off' will be perceived as 'off'. Actively love your partner enough to understand politics and perceptions, and honor her in both.

- Do not give to another woman anything, be it physical, mental, spiritual or emotional, that otherwise belongs to your wife or girlfriend. This is the most important rule (and easiest to follow). Cheating is not just intercourse; it is the betrayal of entering into *any congress of the human experience designed to be enjoyed between man and wife.*

These things, Modern Knight, are not heavy burdens. Are not legalistic. Are not 'punching a checklist.' Rather, they are the natural outflow of love. And love loves, actively and intentionally.

CHAPTER 18
ON CRYSTALS, ASTROLOGY, AND LYING

It's imperative to understand that although this book provides 'profiling', educating, calling out, categorizing and documenting help tips for those potentially in the clutches of a Psychic Vampire and is by nature of emphasis *negative*, the day-to-day quality of the relationship *is not awful,* and may actually feel, for the most part, *quite good,* or even *great.* It is not intended that the reader create a mind-picture of chronic fighting, verbal abuse, terror or persistent negativity, for this is not so.

The Prey is fed upon slowly: here a little, there a little.

The Man-Hater rant-fests don't occur oft, but when they do, they are noteworthy. The pressure to share the *'family bed'* with her eleven-year-old doesn't happen every time; in fact sometimes the Vampire coordinates a sleepover so that you *can* enjoy some intimacy. The handholds have reduced, sure, but they are still present. The art of the handwritten note that caused you to fall deeply and irreparably in love with her still occur, albeit sparingly.

Laughing and cutting up over a comedy film – yes, still there too. Enjoyable fellowship over meal and wine? Happening yet. Sunset walks and date-tennis? Yes, still occurring as well.

The positive side or upswing of the rollercoaster must be pointed out, as this is precisely what makes it a rollercoaster. The yo-yo must go down, as well as up, and then down again. Likewise must the Quiet Man replenish his essence and energy. He must make more blood in order to supply more blood.

For what the Vampire has created is neither an overtly negative environment, which would be self-defeating (as the Prey would leave, removing her supply), nor a positive environment, which would result in her starvation (for a positive, calm, warm environment doesn't gestate the energy she needs). Rather, the mood and tenor is one of slow-building heaviness, of creeping denial and progressive doubt that leads either to *The Discard* at conclusion (she leaves him), or the transformation of a virile, masculine, energetic, strong and fun man into a defeated, empty, emasculated Quiet Man that she collects and shelves while she moves onto the next one via serial infidelity (she remains with him).

The process is slow; paper cuts, not gashes. The oven requires but a little gas, and too much wood burns the chicken. It is doubt, fear, and insecurity combined with the periodic, and gloriously delicious, outburst or crazy-making response that gives her blood for the letting, a feast upon the cornucopia of his soul.

Her real and true self you will never know. The positive version of her is an act – a mask worn to fatten the calf. The negative version of her is also an act, a mask worn to paw the mouse.

The hard truth is that she does not love the Quiet Man. *Love is a choice, and she chooses not to love you.* The function of the relationship is to play out her vengeance upon the one who did not requite her love; a punishment of the entire gender for the sake of the army boy who spurned her and the town that dared try and contain and label her.

So, for each and every day the Quiet Man has known her, behind the mask has she lived.

Her sorry condition has resulted in the formation of a horrible custom. A runaway train that cannot be stopped until it fully derails, crashing wholly from the tracks. She has become a habitual, chronic liar.

This does not necessitate that she is lying to the Quiet Man (yet); rather, as her mask inevitably slips, her character and nature manifest. And with the manifestation, his concerns and observations fall logically upon this thought: *If she snickers and lies about why she missed a lunch date with her girlfriend, is she snickering and lying about me to others?*

Three noteworthy examples follow about the Psychic Vampire and a slowly brewing home culture of lying.

1. She brings you in on her small 'white lies' to make you feel exclusive, and part of her schemes

The self-diagnosed introvert has a secret – and you, her love-stricken partner, have been exclusively invited to be part of it.

Although known for her honest character, selfless sweetness, and childlike, flower-childesque innocence on matters worldly, when at home, brooding on her corner of the couch, the unicorn becomes a wasp, her sting of derogatory slander unleashed upon all around her. In the common vernacular, *the Femme Vampire is a 'shit-talker'*. She works in insults and put-downs the way Picasso worked with oils and acrylics.

The moment she crosses the door and her blazer alights upon the floor, she descends as an angry helicopter upon her lounging spot. The corner of the couch is her lair, a den where only vipers might find comradery and welcome. Her slender fingers clutch and clasp her evening coffee; her pupils transform to slits; her sweet, perfectly symmetrical lush lips become a sewer of rank hatred for any humans that dared cross her or deeply disrupted her day simply by existing.

The 'shy introvert' unleashes hell on everyone and everything, ranging from the guy who talked too long during a conference call and the supervisor whose level of ignorance should disqualify him from being allowed to live another day, to even her mother, who is overweight and simply won't stop posting on social media about the weather or her church.

That such a beautiful water sprite can utter the words of an ogre in the shadows of your living room may, primarily due to shock value, be viewed as comedic the first few times (*she's just having a bad day*). By visceral insult session nine hundred, however, 'tis not cute but ugly, unhealthy and off-putting.

As with her now increasing vulgar washroom habits, her belching and gross obsession with bowel movements, she, possessing brilliance in her malevolence, knows this too is off-putting, and hopes to raise your stress and concern on one hand, and take pleasure if perchance you join her in the behavior on the other.

Note – never join your partner, work colleague or any other person speaking ill of others in secret. The things that come forth from your mouth will be weaponized against you by those encouraging your involvement in such things.

But the Quiet Man does love her, does enjoy sitting with her after work, is delighted and thankful to sit watching TV or enjoying tea with her and, as much as he can navigate the situation without fully degenerating into her realm of ripping others to shreds, lightly goes along with it.

This is the reality of how the evening goes. He is not going to become her judge, lecture her on being nice to one's neighbor, or self-righteously leave the room. Nay; he will laugh at some of the comments, nod in acquiescence at times, and softly redirect to lighter banter where possible.

Then cometh the lies.

After an eloquent session about how her best friend (you know, the one who is her ex-husband's live-in girlfriend):

- Is annoying
- Is pesky
- Is clingy
- Dresses too much like the Vampire
- Copied her nail color
- Talks about work too much
- Mismanages her finances
- Is too materialistic

- Calls too often
- Doesn't call often enough
- Is selfish
- Has mental issues

She then turns directly to you and asks you to commit a lie.

"Lover, if she asks, we are both out of town up in Flagstaff this weekend and have no cell service. OK?"

Like the first cancer cell present in the body, the smallest lies are the most lethal; not in distance but direction. For each begets another, and another.

Next she bids you lie about which friends she was with to avoid this friend or that one, or directly tells you braggadocio tales about the three ways she convinced her manager that her work was completed when it wasn't. How she claimed she was on a view-only video presentation when she was in reality at the mall and a myriad of other fibs, white lies and 'doozies' that ultimately reveal the pattern of a person who lies and lies, often for their own sake!

2. She lies to her children.

Though one can stomach their spouse or partner fibbing about matters with co-workers and girlfriends, the red flag shoots up the flagpole as a launching rocket when the habitual lying concerns her own children.

The Vampire resents having a child at all, and the lass or lad are a nuisance at best – but more often a political pawn to both punish and remain connected to her ex, and to be used as an object that makes the Vampire publicly look like 'Mom of the Year' (even though she hasn't cooked a healthy meal for the kid in over three years).

When the Vampire encourages you to participate in a lie or cover-up concerning her own seed, some part of the world dies. Flowers droop, trees leave and deserts crackle. It's offensive to the core.

"Honey, please don't tell my daughter we went to Disneyland without her. Don't post any pictures from the trip. We'll take her next year." Or "My darling, don't tell her but I hate her shoes."

Beyond the obvious complex 'lose-lose' scenarios this levies upon the gentleman, the shock factor is tremendous. Most adults understand that you should never, as an absolute, lie to children. They can absorb hard truths. They can understand that they weren't included in a fun outing 'this time', but will be when older or on another occasion.

Lying to a child:

- Teaches and prepares them to lie (for what lie or sin is never ultimately brought to light?)
- Exposes them to the truth that the parent does not respect them enough to be honest
- Coddles them in fantasy and untruth, arresting them on the journey to becoming honest, high-functioning adults.

The conservative-but-sort-of-witchy, sort-of-hippie, ultra-sexy goddess you fell in love with has allowed the mask to slip, revealing a farting, nasty, slanderous and hate-filled woman who lies and lies and lies; the beauty revealing she is the beast.

A beast... with fangs.

3.   She Poses as a New Age Guru but can't name one crystal.

The Vampire hates her coworkers.

She deeply dislikes her best friend (you know, the one she shares at least one penis with).

She lies to her children.

And lastly, she is simply not the person she claims to be; even her hobbies and interests are facades.

As a gentleman and Modern-Day Knight, you are responsible for taking an active, supportive interest in your partner's interests. She suffers your football and fishing; you can invest time in the things that bring her joy, and not just via lip-service or half-hearted, half-eared gestures and passing conversations.

What does she like? What brings her joy? How can you support, encourage, and participate in (or choose to not participate in, if the activity or interest is something she enjoys for her time alone) the things she likes?

Being interested, available, present, and supportive are choices. For love loves.

Imagine, however, the shock of exercising these *active love skill-sets*, listening intently, demonstrating an appetite for learning, creating a forum for her to show off and shine, and then the following happens...

Quiet Man: "I don't know much about the healing properties of crystals, but I'm fascinated by your knowledge and love of the subject. Which ones are good for chronic knee pain?"

Psychic Vampire: "I don't know."

Quiet Man: "Ah, well, can this one help with the flow of energy in our living room? I like the blue color."

Psychic Vampire: "I've not heard that one mentioned on the podcast I listen to. You just have to sense and feel such things."

Quiet Man: "OK, Lover! I thought each crystal had a specific benefit to each room in the home. You're the expert; which should we get for our bathrooms?"

Psychic Vampire: "I'm an empath and just know via intuition and feelings which ones to use."

As with the other attributes, character flaws, red flags and games covered hitherto, it is most often men that do the above. Men feign knowledge about cars – until you need them to fix one, or make a knowledgeable purchase. Men tout their political chest-thumping prowess, but cannot articulate how a bill becomes a law. Men claim to be experts at everything and probably haven't read a book since they were forced to in grade school.

Here the Psychic Femme Vampire has once again borrowed from what men do, and perfected it in her own craft. She has created a persona, and indeed an entire caricature, built upon falsehood and deception.

Although she can try to hide behind buzzwords like 'empath', 'feelings over knowledge' and 'intuition', it is patently dishonest to walk around upon the Earth professing to have subject-matter expertise or content knowledge of something when you do not.

Feigned shyness doth not a liar unmake.

Even Natural Witches and Druids study the names, classifications, properties and uses of herbs for decades and decades...

CHAPTER 13
THE HOUSE WASN'T HAUNTED... SHE WAS

So maybe she doesn't know that onyx is believed to combat grief or that topaz is suggested to improve thyroid issues. And maybe she's never read the Druid's Prayer – and so what if she doesn't know that yoga is a Hindu religious exercise meant to access the Kundalini Snake spirit that they believe is coiled within the base of each person's spine?

She needs not know these things to be *spiritual*. In most instances, the command of a few buzzwords coupled with selected attire and a projected vibe will suffice to fool many. And where the strategy calls for the Femme Vampire to don more of a Christian façade, the form of spirituality turns to the realm of the occultic and the demonic. This is especially so if her Quiet Man candidate has a professed faith or follows any form of Christianity.

Spiritual trauma is potent; a satisfying elixir to the Covert Narc (for spiritual abuse is just as real and damaging as emotional, mental and physical abuse).

The impact of an actual paranormal event or haunting on a couple could and should be the topic of a separate work but will be touched upon lightly here. Although many perceived hauntings are the result of emotional trauma, drug use, or mental illness, when the incident/situation is real, the results are devastating and life-altering.

Where the couple are believers, the following may ensue:

- Chronic arguing caused by exhaustion: when the couple are nightly dealing with something going 'bump in the night', manifestations partially seen down the hall, crockery moving itself in the kitchen etc., the effect is exhaustion. Three hours a night of interrupted and fearful sleep is not sustainable. From exhaustion comes grumpiness, and from grumpiness, edgy, argumentative overtures in the home.

- Never alone to be alone: couples require a safe, private place that is *all theirs*. As covered with respect to the sanctity and import of a nighttime routine between adults, a thriving couple requires time apart from children, relatives, friends... and demons. When constantly sharing space with their 'unwanted visitor', intimacy and unity suffers.

- Emasculation of the Man who can't 'fix it': Dad can kill a snake in the yard. Hubby can wrestle a drunken robber to the floor in the grocery store. But you can't stab a spirit, neither punch a demon. As Men are accountable to be protectors in their homes, a shame and embarrassment is born of a haunting, as all eyes look to the dad/husband (equally afraid and helpless) who is unable to get 'the Shadow Man out of the attic'. This can result, when paired with exhaustion from nightly paranormal harassment, in the wife or children starting to distrust or even accuse the man of failing in other areas. "You can't fix the haunting; can you really fix our financial struggles? Can you really pay the mortgage? Overcome your mean boss? Not get fired and land us in the streets?"

The most charming, loving and warm families turn on one another in this uniquely harrowing experience. For believers, the purpose and function of a haunting or demonic situation is for the Devil to render the couple ineffectual in their faith. Their salvation is not at risk, but their example to the lost, their joy, and their walk 'down here' certainly is.

Where the couple are non-believers but spiritual, the terror, fear, harassment and otherworldly abuse is similar, but the objective differs.

- Early in the haunting, the Man feels compelled to try magical words, amulets or other methods to vanquish the demon. These early efforts meet with success, and the man is viewed as an invincible hero to his wife/partner. A demon slayer, a demi-god!
- However, the early success is a ploy, and the 'thing' comes back sevenfold fierce and enraged each time.
- Instead of seeing his need for God's provision, the Man, filled with pride and growing shame, goes further and further into the Occult (or heretical Christianity), seeking solutions for the problem.
  - He has a shaman cleanse the home;
  - Although not a Catholic or Anglican believer, he tries it out and has priests put magical water about the entryways or brings other idols into the home;
  - He conducts a seance to try and contact the unwanted visitor and reason with it.
- All the while, his partner may be recommending and executing similar methods in an attempt to vanquish the entity.
- The sleeplessness, strife, anger, fear and ultimately hatred of one another intensifies.

The unbelieving but spiritual couple seek out and trust everything but God, often turning to the very source of the problem to solve the problem. When you see tormented, chronically fatigued New Agers bouncing from seminar to seminar, ever miserable, skin becoming grey and pale, pray for them, as they may be wrestling with this sort of problem privately at home.

For believers, the strategy is to **keep them ineffective.**

For non-believing spiritual folks, the strategy is to **keep them lost in religion, custom or ritual.**

Lastly, for atheists there are of course no hauntings, no demonic oppression, no supernatural events of any kind. Why would there be? The last thing Satan would ever do is prompt someone who believes in *nothing* to experience *something*. For if they did, be it bad or good, they might start asking difficult worldview questions, or even run straight to the Lord, seeking His help.

The Psychic Vampire is well-read, an adept at the wiles of the Devil. The same things he and his agents do to steal, kill and destroy families and individuals, she will bottle and likewise do. In this regard, her playbook is similar.

If her Quiet Man is a Christian, she may:

- Insist there are evil spirits in the home
- Make convincing arguments that the energy of the home is impacting the relationship
- Plant evidence of hauntings (upside-down crosses etc.)
- Take advantage of a real incident and make it a nightly visitation. (For example, the couple may experience a spooky night where both truly believe something evil is in the home. She feasts on the fear and negative energy from it, then insists it has returned, again and again)
- Use a real or manufactured incident to insist that the Quiet Man's views of God and the church are false because 'whatever he is doing to get rid of it isn't working'

Meanwhile, the Vampire is not a Christian, so behind the scenes she begins to slander the Quiet Man to her friends (you know, the ones she actually hates and slanders to the Quiet Man in her angry daily after-work routine). Whilst creating and/or taking advantage of a dark, unsettling situation at home, she is:

- Telling her friends that he is crazy
- Telling her friends that he is a religious nut
- Telling her friends that he is possessed
- Mocking the faith of her partner

If her Quiet Man is not a Christian, but possesses some spirituality or belief, she will run him through an exhausting cycle of every possible religion, cult, practice, and superstition. He will be made to join her in having a new god every week, even if the composite gathering and amalgamation of diverse religious world-views are contradictory, incompatible and frankly insulting to each and every one of them.

The veracity or validity of the belief won't matter – only the fact that she and he are doing 'something spiritual' to chase away the demons.

Each of these flirtatious fads with shamans, priests, goddesses and witchdoctors will of course lead only to more hauntings, more chaos, and more distress. The end state will be a Quiet Man who no longer possesses an anchor to any cohesive belief system; a hole-riddled leaf blowing in the wind without spiritual passion, conviction or wisdom.

An empty soul is easy to control, which greatly pleases the Psychic Vampire.

Mirroring the strategy of the Father of Lies, with respect to atheists, the Vampire will concoct no hauntings, summon no Shadow Men or Night Hags; nothing untoward going 'bump in the night'. Theirs will be a house of *science* where spirituality is reduced to feelings and intuitions on how to live in the 'now', *for the now is all there is for those whose destiny is simply to become a dirt sandwich.*

And the Psychic Vampire has a myriad of other tools she can deploy to feed upon a home that embraces that empty, false worldview.

CHAPTER 20
TWO KINGS AND NO QUEEN

Genesis 3:16, KJV: "Unto the woman he said, I will greatly multiply thy sorrow and thy conception; in sorrow thou shalt bring forth children; and thy desire shall be to thy husband, and he shall rule over thee."

For six thousand years, a self-evident and sometimes intense tension has raged amongst the genders. Scripture teaches, observation validates, and personal honesty and sincerity quadruple confirms (the Bible, being God's word, matches observable reality repeatedly) that this is so.

Men are accountable for being leaders in the relationship, but the Fall tends to make us tyrants instead of good leaders. We overreach; we control; we know we are supposed to lead, but we don't quite know how. We are insecure.

Something in our nature tells us that there was a divinely ordained symbiotic relational order. When a couple are 'in the groove' and things are going well, we sometimes (though too rarely) see this in action. There are hints and remnants of how it ought to be, only we bungle it up and fall short every day.

This is our fallen nature.

Likewise, Women are to nurture, support, serve as a compatible helpmate for their Men.

Yet, consistent with the account of the Fall, women instead usurp the man; undermine the man; resent the man; abandon their own nature and instead desire to be as the man.

Men have a tendency to be tyrants. Women have a tendency to want to rebel against tyranny and then... become the tyrant. This woeful condition is the backdrop that we as sinful, flawed men and women face every day.

When in love and accountable, men seek to win the battle on more days than they lose it through:

- Servant leadership, not dictatorship, using Christ as the example
- Accountability-based leadership
- Sacrificial leadership
- Consensus-driven leadership (for Scripture is also clear that Man and Woman are to submit themselves one to another; 'tis not just the Woman doing the submitting)[7]
- Unity-based leadership

In short: *Men, yes, be the leader, be a strong leader, be a manly man, just don't be a jerk about it!*

In healthy relationships, both partners understand that there are subtle, nuanced gender stressors and conflicts that can be quite difficult to sort out.

But healthy couples:

1. Recognize that our identity is as individuals first, not groups (i.e. you are a person first, not a gender, race, sexual orientation etc.)

2. Recognize that the two individuals that make up the 'team' (marriage, relationship etc.) are under Grace, not Law, and can customize their team to function in whatever way is productive for them, provided they don't deny reality or nature in customizing their approach.

3. And lastly that, yes, there *are* genders norms and differences.

Because their priority and approach matches reality, highly successful couples need not discuss 'gender topics' frequently, if ever. "Gender stressors are real; we are mature enough to understand the reality of them, but wise enough not to drone on about them day after day after day. We focus on loving each other, not who ought to do this or that."

---

7 Ephesians 5:21

By contrast, the Psychic Femme Vampire can't let a day go by without concocting a reason to promote feminism and make gender identity topics the daily agenda – every day. This would be analogous to the grumpy father who finds cause to tell his children "I'm the Dad and you WILL obey me" three hundred and nine times per day.

In the same way that the children understand who the Dad is in their family organizational chart, likewise does the angry and bitter Vampire not need declare her liberation and dependence every two to three hours.

Here there does seem to be a sequence of events:

- Strange spiritual events, hauntings or experiences occur in the home on an ongoing chronic basis
- The situation brings about discussions regarding the Biblical roles and offices for men and women
- The exhaustion from the haunting or spiritual stress causes conflict, and tendencies for the extreme (e.g. the man declares "I'm the boss, damn it!", and thus sentences himself to a life of condemnation from the Vampire for his indiscretion).

The Psychic Vampire is a woman who carries a broken heart, loathes her small-town upbringing and, above all, was seduced and mentored by a woman (or women) with a worldview devoted to the destruction of masculinity as an extension and collateral loss of its hatred for the Creator. She has been poisoned by a political ideology, and the warped lens through which she sees the world has her wanting to be as a man and paradoxically hating women (especially mothers and motherhood).

As a result, she must constantly remind the man that she will:

- Not be controlled (translation: he will neither make nor propose any decision)
- Not be belittled (translation: disagreed with)
- Not be berated (translation: he must not so much as look at her sideways)

She will remind him again and again:

- They are Co-CEOs
- They are Co-Popes
- They are Two Heads
- They are Two Kings

That he in fact does not strut around being a tyrannical jerk, and that he feels a great God-given drive to physically protect her and a natural drive to work hard and provide for her that is being disrupted, diminished, and devalued by her constant attacks on his manhood, is irrelevant. She will stir gender strife until he submits, then leave him for being weak.

This is amongst her favorite strategies: delicious morsels for the narcissist's feast.

As a structure more consistent with western civilization gives way to her vision of genderless 'equitable' beings splitting the lease and wearing matching flannels ensues, it is not just manhood that suffers – it is womanhood.

Common-sense questions arise:

- Why would anyone WANT to pay the bills?
- Why would anyone WANT to do physical hard labor?
- Why would anyone intentionally deny the respect of an open door, or waiting to eat until she is seated and ready?

The woman is the glory of the man. She goes first. He protects and honors her.

He must work. She can choose to work or not to work.

If they cannot reach consensus on an extremely difficult decision, she supports his final say. For he answers to God for the overall quality and success of the team, not her.

She is graceful, organized, and nurturing; she has gifts and skill-sets he will never possess, just as he has gifts and skill-sets she will never possess.

The kingdom needs a King AND a Queen to prosper.

The hatred of men and manhood demands – like a vicious circle that revolts against the laws of nature and nature's God as it turns, like a cyclone – hatred of womanhood as well. In this regard, the Psychic Vampire opposes herself. This leaves her hating all gender roles, all distinctions between Man and Woman, all relationships of any sort that resemble those used as pillars and bedrocks of western civilization. And the functional outworking of her 'Two Kings' model of course becomes 'One King', which in the end is her.

This brings about the near fulfillment of her quest to create of her mate the Quiet Man; a defeated, emasculated soul who is clipped and snipped. A eunuch without role, job or purpose on the team. Her other strategies, executed with surgical precision, have taught him that any response is 'crazy', any protest is 'control', and any backlash or assertion earns him her favorite label, 'narcissist'.

CHAPTER 21
YOU DESERVE TO BE PICKED UP FROM THE AIRPORT

The reader might have noticed that the past several chapters have been shy on advice or recommendations on 'what to do about it'. This is not by oversight or accident, as there is neither coaching nor comfort to be found when the woman you adore is assaulting your faith or your manhood.

These are 'no-fly zones' or 'off-limits areas' and when they are insulted, berated, attacked or disparaged, the most important thing to note is that these are not the ends in and of themselves. Rather, they are part of a process, and something far worse is coming.

The Discard.

Note the term – and if you are reading this work somewhere between the Intentional Taboos, the increasing and seemingly pointless serial lying and 'the haunting', then you have the benefit of forewarning.

The Barn is on fire.

The Sky is falling.

The Discard is coming.

If flipping these pages after, then the benefit is support via shared experience and lessons gleaned from the value that is hindsight.

The Discard is coming. But it is not here yet...

Before the Vampire can throw you away with the rubbish, she has to first attempt to cause you to feel *as rubbish*. And this she will accomplish, drawing down the mask gradually to reveal reptilian slits behind hazel eyes and ghastly, skeletal cheekbones beneath her tanned, opaque, and healthy-looking skin.

She tires of wearing the mask. She desires to feed in the open, unencumbered by pretense or pretext.

And thus she begins by destroying every cute ritual, every nuanced romantic routine, taking a sledgehammer to the foundation of all you thought you were during the courtship and (then) love-bombing stages.

The way you serve her French toast is not only no longer appreciated and met with a smile that could light a great city during a power outage: it is met with dismissive criticism about how one side is burnt, how the lingonberries are too tart, or how she actually never really fancied French toast after all.

The way you massage her bad shoulder, seeking and destroying her knots with the love-radar built into your fingertips, is now met with complaints that you are too rough, too soft or that your technique really doesn't help her and actually hurts, though nothing has changed in your passionate approach and your methods have actually improved over the many months via practice and familiarity with her form.

The dismantling of the great or neat things that you thought you had, or were, is then compounded when she simply stops doing things. And moreover, ridicules that which she once did.

For example:

During the months that you dated, but before you lived together, you flew from another state to spend countless hours laughing, shopping, dining and making out with her. When you traveled, not having a car in her home town, she would greet you at the airport.

Being great communicators, you openly discussed the deep, deep value and honor of this. When a loved one ascends 35,000 feet into the heavens and hazards their lives (four, five or six times a month), there is little greater honor than being there to greet them when they arrive.

This has little to do with romance and is a precept and principle extended by most adults in a business, family or friendship setting. If someone is flying to you, pick them up. This is basic, important and special. You both agreed with this principle. You both executed this principle. It is easy; it is not burdensome; it is as natural as opening a door, carrying a heavy object or any other of the myriad millions of polite things individuals do to express respect, affection or love.

As with other topics, this one is so basic that, beyond extending gratitude and thanksgiving, the matter isn't discussed; *you just do it*. She just did it.

Until she didn't.

After living together for months, the Quiet Man has work travel and is gone for a week. Upon his return, very much looking forward to her embrace near the baggage claim carousel, he is instead met with a text that may read like this:

"Welcome home, honey. Just get a taxi to the house. I'm an introvert and just not up for dealing with the people at the airport."

The 'introvert' had no such barriers the nineteen prior times she met you at the airport. She wasn't 'too shy' the three times she met you with a blockbuster-movie-level kiss and a handwritten note. What has changed?

The change is this. The Psychic Vampire has chosen to show you that she never wanted to do such things; she does not respect you enough to choose to drive to the airport; she thinks such things are unimportant, lame or cliché.

Fangs revealed, she awaits your response.

As the Quiet Man attempts to process what has transpired – the destruction of tradition, the wounds of deep disrespect – and contemplates how and if to respond, let him remember that *love is a choice*. Love loves, daily. The things you do for her that she likes in month 1, do also with effort and conviction in month 401.

Likewise, **YOU DESERVE TO BE PICKED UP FROM THE AIRPORT!**

You are not a controlling jerk for expecting to be treated consistently. You are not a narcissist for expecting to be treated with respect and romance. You can protest. You can declare your worth.

By the time she stops picking you up at the airport, you must comprehend hard truths:

- She is picking someone else up at the airport while you are away.
- She is still penning those wondrous handwritten missives – only not to you.
- You are now the object of the slanderous rant fests with her sister and friends.
- At this point, she does not love you.

This final point is the most sticking, and most poignant. Your pathway, Modern Knight, to being a thriving, healed, fully actualized and responsible victor and not a sniveling victim lies not in diagnosing her daddy issues, calling her a narcissist, or declaring that she was made this way or that way and cannot change. Whether any of these factors be true or untrue, how are they relevant?

Love loves. Love chooses to love, actively, with effort and sacrifice every day.

You are not a victim healing from abuse. You are a wounded warrior dealing with the simple fact that someone you love does not in turn love you. That empowers you to return from this and not lose five to ten years being damaged by it.

A person loves who they love. And she does not love you.

Sometimes a person who chooses not to love recaptures their love, finds their way back, is convicted of their wrongs and does restore their active love. The key for the Modern Knight is to never compromise on his value but to simultaneously give the Vampire space and grace to recover herself and choose to love again.

But hold out no hope for the same. When she stops picking you up at airports, the end is likely nigh, and the key is to NOT become a groveling Quiet Man in a vain effort to extend the inevitable. Rather it is to remember who you are, to not answer evil with evil or strife with strife, and to start to prepare yourself to be honorable in a situation where a monster is about to feast upon, devour, and then yes, **DISCARD** your heart.

The discard is indeed nigh, and one glaring loud sign of the Last Trumpet of your Love remains...

CHAPTER 22
FIRST THOUGHT, LAST THOUGHT.
IF SHE CHANGES THAT, YOU'RE FUCKED

Paying no mind to sappiness or allegations of 'too many rom-coms', let us now go on to the furthest realms of brutal honesty.

Each of us have one person we think of when we rise and when we repose. In the happy moments wrestling between wakefulness and sleep, she visits us. When we wrestle to redeem three more winks ere the dawn or alarm reminds us with unwelcome light or shrill sound that another day of stress, pressure and cruelty in a brutal world awaits – she is there, offering, in the world of dreams, respite, fantasy and hope.

For he who can but roll over and touch the woman that delightfully haunts his dreams, his are the riches of the world, though he be destitute!

Perhaps an old gentleman is a widow and she, his first and last thought, fuels the otherwise bitter day, rendering it the opposite of lonely; for he knows she ever awaits his resting and waking thoughts, day by day, to remind him of what was, and what might be again.

Or your first and last thought may be a damsel of youth whose grandeur hewed a hole in your chest none can ever fill. For you loved her in an instant and through the years, be it right or wrong, for good or ill, you cleave unto her, and love her still.

If we lose a love by divorce or by decease and life peradventure grants a new First and Last, we are of all men most blessed, for how often does actual love grace man? Once? Twice? Whatever the count decreed, the number is few, and by this measure do you know love: that every day without fail she is your first thought and your last thought, and on the morrow, your first thought again!

Oh, you had a quarrel? Still Last Thought and First Thought.

Ah, she is not considered the most comely in the class – yet First Thought, Last Thought.

You don't like her parents – Last Thought, First Thought.

You hate her politics! First Thought, Last Thought

You've not seen her in ten years – Last Thought, First Thought.

You love her; this is how you know. Deny it not and embrace the truth of it. And by the by, to honor women that may come into your life, do not date until your dreamtime visitor removes Cupid's Arrow and passes it to another – or you might become as the subject of this book.

For what is the Psychic Vampire but one who has allowed a broken heart to be used by sociopathic elites that are devoid of love? Is she a victim? No. At times a pawn of an intentional cultural system that mocks love? Aye.

And because one who has experienced First Thought, Last Thought knows it is the paramount gauge for his or her own love, he or she has the common sense and discernment to know when it is lost. Either when they lose it or when their partner has lost it – for them.

Diverting for a moment into the circular challenge of the matter with strong words to the Modern-Day Knight: *if you choose to actively love every day it becomes not just a habit, but a joy; and the reward, both of its own merit and her reciprocity, will not fade, neither will she cease to be your First Thought, Last Thought.*

You cannot help with whom you fall in love, but First Thought, Last Thought is not just a product of the falling, but rather the fruits of the efforts of love. If you invest 110% into the Lovebank, and she 110% for her part as well, then First Thought and Last Thought she shall ever remain!

'Tis left for the rest of us who have lost in love to truly dream, speculate, and wish for what can be wrought through hard work, investment and the 'luck' or 'chance' that it is invested in kind.

Returning now to the Femme Vampire. Again, it must be remembered that the whole of her constitution is one of intent, deep-rooted knowledge, and willful hurts. This book is now about those who fall out of love, and do so honorably, or lose interest and have their cause. It is not about those who are slightly mean or rather lazy, or just who, in the end, sorta liked someone else.

This is a book rather about the 0.0001% who are actual monsters roaming the countryside with full command of the impact of First and Last thoughts and who then withdraw it... purposefully.

You will not feel a fade-out. You will be blissfully enjoying the communication and love-language rituals with your partner and then one day, randomly, she will engage you in a battle designed to make you feel badly about the fact that you talk too much, text too romantically, or are too intense in your words.

The very woman who complimented you a thousand and nine times for your Shakespearean text prose, who celebrated you as the 'one guy who gets it', will suddenly and inexplicably annihilate all of that and abruptly and spontaneously act like the lazy boyfriend who simply can't be bothered to take a call or send a text.

The Quiet Man will be confused, bewildered and angry.

As she systematically cancels everything good and great and fun and warm about the foundations of your relationship, a desperation will ensue as you realize that, if those things were nothing, then you and she have nothing, and your relationship is... nothing.

She wants you to feel this way. She needs, at this stage, to feed from your nothing. To eat your nothing.

How you handle her not only drastically reducing 'First and Last' but mocking your desperate defense and longing for its return will determine her decision-tree and what happens next.

If you yield to a relationship where:

1. She is the CEO

    Your faith doesn't matter

2. Your nighttime routines are gone

3. You don't object to her bizarre taboos
4. You suffer her 'just inappropriate enough' relationships with other men
5. You stop complaining when she doesn't pick you up from the airport
6. You allow the seven well-constructed "I love you because..." paragraphs at night to become poorly spelled one-line text messages such as 'luv ya' and the morning coffee routine to become a long-ago tradition replaced by nothing...

Then she will put you, along with your testicles, on the mantle. She will keep you for stability, appearances, or financial purposes, and begin/continue her hunt for the next one, and the next.

Under this scenario you become the seventy-nine-year-old alcoholic who stopped living at forty and two and she the yelling, boisterous 'introvert' who acts self-righteously amongst the cousins and grandchildren, though she led a monstrous life of affairs, hypocrisy and abuse, hating everything and everyone connected to a Judeo-Christian or western civilization.

But, if you point out the decline in her investment in your routine, the loss of the polish and shine of your amazing romance, the fading of your life-film together to grey, then you have gifted her one of her final feasts of a different sort.

Hell will be unleashed!

1. Only narcissistic assholes 'keep score'!
2. She is not obligated to put effort into her 'I love yous'!
3. You should be thankful for what you do get and stop referencing the past!
4. You are just a narcissist trying to control how she acts!
5. You complaining about it is the reason she doesn't do it!
6. "It's never enough!"
7. I'm an INTROVERT! (screeching)

After punishing you for daring to rise up and point out well, anything, at this stage, and for not fully coming forth from the cocoon as the Quiet Man, you, my Modern-Day Knight, *will be discarded.*

First and Last Thoughts (and the actions associated with them) diminishing, being ridiculed or ruined, signifies that the end is nigh and cruel, movie-level destruction awaits.

CHAPTER 23
THE DISCARD, FANGS REVEALED

For the man who stood up for himself, challenged inconsistencies, made declaration that he deserved to be done unto as he did unto others; for the fellow who did get baited into a few 'crazy-making responses', being bested by her taboos, ogre-esque belching and lewd bathroom banter, and was increasingly and righteously angry over her soft adultery and chronic lies, battling her over it from time to time; for the one who resisted, with varying degrees of success, becoming The Quiet Man...

The Discard Cometh.

Note that the relationship never featured, not once:

- Name-calling
- Insults of one's appearance (weight, height, shape, etc.)
- Deep, deep insults or degrading words and actions aimed at achieving an obvious 'point of no return'

The term *gaslighting*, though surely over-used and often mis-used, has no superior substitute for describing the subtle, piecemeal chipping away at all that was good about who you were – and if the Vampire had her druthers, your sanity besides.

The Resisting Man, who would not yield to the Quiet Man, of course noticed the gradual decline of the quality of the partner-ship – the steady pinging in the ears and the jolt in the gut that said this would not be forever. But the *good times still appeared now and again as well.*

The lovemaking was still epic. Romantic outings yet abounded. The air in the home was still filled periodically with rib-splitting laughter, music and merriment. (After all, she is a vampire; she nibbles and punctures surgically – she does not maul and gorge.) A kernel of foundational love persisted, at least in the perception of the Quiet Man candidate, and the majority thought was that the vase was cracked, not shattered.

But when he protested his version of the airport pickup or railed as a warrior against the diminishing of goodnights and good mornings, it was only a matter of time before the vase would be obliterated, crushed to dust, and then – nothingness!

The Discard typically begins via text or social media. She will wait until you are away on a trip, visiting family, or otherwise far removed from 'her space'. People can be especially cruel behind a keyboard or mobile device, keystrokes equal in impact to a knife or a gun.

On the appointed day of his comeuppance and judgement, the Resisting Man will say one thing, rather innocuous, which gives her license to trigger her plan. Things you never say, type, intimate or even think about a loved one (or anyone) start.

The very first blow hits; shock and awe ensue.

- "You're a fucking bastard" (Note that she has never spoken this way before)
- "My mother warned me that you were a serial loser" (Her mother appeared to have loved you and even preferred your company to hers)
- "You're fat"
- "You're a faggot"
- "I don't love you, do NOT come home"
- "Trailer trash"

Any response is met with ferocious texting about how you need to stop responding to her right now! When you cease responding, she resumes overt, visceral and deep hatred.

- "Your good morning routine is STUPID!"
- "Your compliments are meaningless!"
- "My friends hate you!"

The shy bunny-rabbit of an introvert expostulates with such extroverted violence that you can actually hear the keys screaming as though an Irish Banshee, wailing the siren of death.

You cannot form spittle in your mouth, which is now dry and as a wasteland.

You cannot reason. You cannot cry your way out of it. She will not take your calls.

If you return insult for insult, she calls you a narcissist and says you have "mommy and self-esteem issues". If you return reason and grace for insult, the enlightened feminist suddenly favors the words 'faggot' and 'pussy'.

You are confused.

Second one: "Right-wing chauvinistic fascist pig!"

Second two: "Baby ass-faggot!"

This is not a quarrel. Nor is it a debate. She is done with you, and she is punctuating it through extreme overkill: the woman you loved the most at once treating you the worst you've ever been treated.

It is not a break-up aimed at a make-up or even a deferred 'fake-up'. Sorry, no. She has made it clear that she has already arranged for your things to be boxed and shipped and that she has no desire to ever see you, hear from you, or even think on you again.

This is not a bluff, neither a fight technique. When the turkey is devoured at Thanksgiving, does the family stare long at the bones, or give a passing thought over the carcass?

Nay. When consumed is the prey, the carcass is... discarded.

She has consumed the sum of the energy she needs from you. Your one true love views you as rubbish and surely already long ago moved to the next Quiet Man candidate.

Much of what she said was confusing, detailed, and mysteriously intrusive, to include blow-by-blow recaps of every pet name, romantic gesture and nice thing you did to, with or for your ex-wife or girlfriend. In addition to the abrupt cessation of life as you knew it, there is an overwhelming violation and intrusion seeping into your being.

When insulting me, how did she know every past sin or mistake I've ever made?

How did she know secret, deeply private things about me?

Did someone help her with this destructive break-up? How does she know things from ten years ago? Is she really psychic?!

No, she is not psychic in that sense... but she is part of a cult – a small-town Psychic Femme Vampire Cult.

CHAPTER 24
IF YOU'RE OVER 35
AND FROM A SMALL TOWN,
DO NOT GO FISHING IN THE SAME OLD POND

After The Discard process – which may last a day or two, or be elongated over a few weeks of (primarily) text-based, heartless cruelty – concludes, the Modern-Day Knight should not evaluate much, and *do* even less.

He finds himself in a hotel room, parent's home, or friend's pull-out sofa, for she (the 'Victim') has threatened him (the 'Narcissist') with every tool of leverage (restraining order, slander to employer, sharing of embarrassing secrets or media content to children or co-workers, etc.) at her disposal to ensure he will not come home. Rather, not go to the place that *was* his home.

His world is now changed.

They are no longer together; the sky has fallen; hopelessness hath set in.

Evaluate not what has happened, for there is logic or reason in it. The only thing the Modern-Day Knight can do at this point is breathe.

Just breathe.

Though at night in bed you feel as if you're trapped in a wetsuit with an anvil on your chest, though you cry until your eyes are crusted and sore and though you curse God by the hour (we are under grace, He understands and grieves with you), do nothing save breathe.

Just breathe.

You will never hold hands with her again.

Just breathe.

You will never pose for selfies at that keen spot outside the museum again.

Just breathe.

You will never teach her about cider, and she will never teach you about wine, ever, ever again.

Just breathe.

Her scent, the one that activates tingles in your toes and fills your whole body with a rush of happiness, you will never again draw into your nostrils.

Just breathe.

You shall never make love to her, shower with her, or kiss her until your lips hurt and your tongue is nigh sprained again. Your ears are ringing, the room is discolored, and you cannot see for the sadness that has enveloped and consumed you. Hard truths confront you and a long, long journey is ahead but now, do nothing. Do nothing save breathe.

Breathe, and DO NOT:

- **Creep her social media.** It will only intensify your hurt and annihilation. There her posts abound with pseudointellectual tripe about introversion and narcissism as she, most ironically, makes the sum of the universal experience about all that she has gone through and desperately gobbles up the attention of those feeding her declaration of victimhood. She is also seducing, flirting with, and pre-courting some one new already (yes, within days).

- **Attempt to contact her in any way.** She has made it clear that you are a "fat, insecure, misogynist, right-wing fag got-ass trailer trash pussy" that she does not love and never wants to see or hear from again. What will attempting to speak with her do but set you up for another beat-down? Don't do it, not even once.

- **Attempt to contact her friends.** This will yield the same result with the exception that they may toy with, give false hope to, or otherwise torture you on her behalf (even though she secretly hates them, as she told you every night after work for three years).
- **Post about it.** Dirty laundry ought never be aired on such a volatile and ofttimes wicked platform. Honor yourself by honoring your privacy and keep social media posts limited to sports, movies, and positive family memories. Keep rants few and break-up content nonexistent. Just go dark online whilst you heal. The reality is that no one will even notice that you're gone for a spell.
- **Self-Harm.**
- **Drink too much.**
- **Drink too little.**
- **Quit your job.**
- **Do anything that may jeopardize your ability to provide for yourself or your family.**

Next, find a tiny circle of support in whom to confide. Rail, cry out and lean upon them, and keep breathing.

Then, after time does what times does, exhale. And in the exhalation, reasoning and reflection will return.

Like a patient who makes a miraculous awakening from a long coma, the Modern-Day Knight sometimes experiences a total recall, realizing he has been through one of these before. For some knights have actually been through these before. It was a decade or more ago, and he loved hard that time too. She was from the same town, had 'escaped', had a military ex-husband, was witchy but conservative, had no children, looked down upon 'kitchen slaves' (women who chose to be homemakers and mothers), had a squeaky little voice and a mean left hook.

After that break-up, he exercised wisdom; not to re-enter the field, neither begin any serious relationships over that long spell. For the Modern-Day Knight would not impose an unrequited love scenario on an unwitting partner; he would not do that which was done unto him, or that which he opposed.

Two years became three and three became seven, and lo, seven became ten – and sure, he dated now and again, but never with purpose or intent. That draining fiasco afore faded into a memory and then out of memory, and he had forgotten all about the *First Vampire* by the time he met and fell in love with the *Second Vampire*.

Lacking a field guide or playbook to manage such things (AKA this book), the romantic gent, now in his fourth decade, was wholly ignorant of:

- The mentor/student model amongst the Small-Town Manhater Cult
- The fact that Femme Narcs share penises and have no qualms with what the rest of us view as "conflicts of interest"
- Something unexpected having happened, with the Resistant Man failing to succumb to the first Succubus's attempt to drain him so many years ago

Standing up or fighting back to a Bully or Abuser causes them to want you, forever. For you are an unfinished meal.

With the first failed relationship, all but forgotten, there was no vicious discard, no vile and violent end. The Mentor erred. When the Resistant Man would not become the Quiet Man, she engaged all the various games and techniques for some final feasts:

- Accusing him of cheating;
- Branding him a narcissist;
- Stealing his church friends even though she had a new god or goddess every five years;
- Physically assaulting him;
- Performing the 'leave and return and leave again' technique.

But he was younger, more brash, had more conviction, and was a skosh cocky – and met her attempts to fang him into Quiet Man submission with equal force and resistance each and every time.

When that break-up occurred it was painful but honorable, because the Vampire and the Modern-Day Knight had locked horns enough to know that they were not a good match and could never be. She may have *been* his life's love, but the current Femme Fatale, the love found at last in his forties when he was more patient, compromising, longsuffering, and temperate, *is* the love of his life and the sum and totality of his focus.

And that lack of focus caused him to miss something very important during the love-bombing, hot-cold undulation and taboos.

When you don't give an abuser or bully that 'final meal', they stay hungry. For days, for months, for years and a decade of years.

The Mentor was herself a Neophyte at that time. She recoiled into shadow, there to read her journals, join her podcasts, immerse and surround herself in all the Fatalistic, Jungian, Secular Humanist and Cultural Marxism she could consume (all the while posing as the darling of the church crowd she beguiled when with him).

The Mentor is a factor in the tale.

A Modern-Day Knight, once in mid-thirties, should not date anyone from his small town. Now, love loves, and the cruelty of the cosmos may force an exception from time to time, but he should certainly not seek out that pool of dating applicants.

The Mentor is THE factor in the tale.

The most important advice or knowledge offered to men who may be in similar circumstance to the examples found on these pages is this: **When you are forty-two, do not date women from your high school.**

The reason we are tempted to do this is certainly rooted in two ignoble aspects of men's nature:

1. **Insecurity**
2. **Laziness**

Firstly, a woman that knew us or knew of us since kindergarten is safe; she poses little risk, less investment and effort. She already knows that we were:

- The high school starting quarterback
- Funny, cute and smart
- Handsome and strong once
- A great leader

The love of youth is a powerful thing. Indeed, this author is of the opinion that the person you love at age fourteen will impact you for the rest of your life (for good, or for ill). And the temptation to go back to the potency of youthful love is great for insecure men. But when forty, finding the Guinevere of our youth is not for us, unfortunately. We must work hard, forge new legends, and invest the effort to make new relationships that are more objective with individuals not able to borrow from a body of data of what we once were. Instead we should find those who peradventure will love us now, as we *are*...

Secondly, we are lazy. It is easy to trawl social media and rekindle a known joke from twenty years ago with a fair damsel of our youth. It is the quickest and least resistant (and less rewarding) path to going backwards in time, rather than forward.

But caution! Even those old female class- and townmates who live thousands of miles apart in the present and are nowhere close (geographically) to that small town they despise, the hillbilly county they loathe, they are far, far more connected than men. They stay in touch, they talk, they instant message, and they may even share a deep-seeded malice towards men... and find in YOU a most delicious target.

The Mentor is THE factor in the tale!

CHAPTER 25
A RETENTION POLICY
FOR OLD TEXT MESSAGES AND EMAILS

How many romantic nicknames exist in the domain of discourse? Fifty? A hundred? Even if thoughtful and creative, the number is few. "Honey"; "Lover Dover"; "Sugar Bear" – there simply are not that many.

But the Mentor kept screenshots of *all of them*. Every text message. Every handwritten note. Every email. Every card.

And when the Mentor connected with her protégé, whether before, during or near the ending of her efforts to make of you the Quiet Man, she shared all of them.

Imagine the intrusiveness and imposition of knowing that two women in their forties are sharing notes about you behind the scenes. That you are lying in bed next to someone who is both violating your privacy and biding her time to judge you with it.

- Sexual comparison notes
- Creative pet and nicknames
- Travel patterns
- Moments of embarrassment
- Achievements
- Parenting style
- Past sins or mistakes

The Mentor may have failed to execute a proper discard, but she will surely prepare her sister in arms not to repeat the error. The Vampire will be equipped in every detail to weaponize things you said, did or wrote... ten years ago.

The main accusation will of course be that you, the Resistant Man, still love this woman from a decade or more ago – that you *targeted* (another favorite term of the Femme Vamps, as every man is a narcissist roaming the countryside, plotting and scheming, targeting his prey) her. That you are playing out the same dysfunction over and over again, that you are a monster, a cheater and a fake.

Each of these accusations are of course a calculated strategy of deflection and, worse, inversion.

Men who have lost in love tend to seek out:

- Women from high school
- Women they didn't know but 'knew of' from their old home town
- Women who are accomplished
- Women who are funny and have a humorous presence on social media
- Women who are seductive, witchy and alluring
- Women who have conservative values and a traditional worldview

'Tis no targeting, profiling or conspiracy, but rather a data-driven reality. That is what we tend to seek, and the Femme Fatale Cult knows this. They are aware, they are brooding, they are connected.

If the man acquiesces to transitioning into the Quiet Man, he may never know that the Vampire chats with his long-ago ex two or three times a week. It is his resistance that gave her cause to bring out the "You called her OTL (*One True Love*) also, didn't you!" or "I know you took her for pho as well."

That the man is actively and consciously re-enacting or recycling some past relationship is contrary to reason and reality. Men are accountable for creating, suggesting, and guiding a high percentage of the outings and events in the relationship. If a man enjoys, for example, massaman curry, he wants to enjoy that which he likes to eat with the person he loves, and also introduce his love to things he likes.

No part of him is thinking:

- *I once took an ex for massaman curry*
- *I had better not take my current partner for massaman curry*
- *In fact, I had better find a new dish to like, as the massaman curry is now connected to my ex*

Such thinking is silly and ridiculous. If a man (or woman) is adjusting what they eat or don't eat based upon what they used to eat with their ex, then THE ADJUSTMENT IS THE BETRAYAL OF THE NEW PARTNER. When a man is in love with a woman, he is not thinking about his ex. He is simply enjoying and savoring life, doing the things he enjoys with his partner. A former spouse is neither precluding nor driving decisions – because she is properly and appropriately not part of his filtering.

But, to the Vampire, doing something remotely similar to what was once done with an ex (of ten years ago) is *cheating* (yet her going on actual dinner outings with someone she bedded down and then friend-zoned is *not cheating*).

That two women conspired together to make your discarding extra detailed, grimy, and in breach of every ethical standard of reasonable behavior amongst adults is an extra twist of the knife in the knight's many wounds. But it again serves as a lesson for triumphing via *not doing it to someone else.*

Here then is a policy with respect to dealing with your current girlfriend or wife's former partners:

- If approached by your lady-love's ex to talk about her past relationship with him, *do not give it place for one second.*
- Their past is their past, and beyond what she may or may not share situationally, it is not your business.
- If he is attempting to 'help you' with red flags, prior sins or 'dirt', then know that:
  - People change
  - Who she was ten years ago is not who she is today
  - The dynamics of their relationship have zilch to do with yours, and once again –

- o It's none of your business
- Likewise, do not reach out to the men that are in a relationship with your ex. This is strange, taboo, *weirdy wolf behavior.* Have honor and let them be.
- Do not intentionally retain scores and scores of texts and emails for the purpose of opportunistic slander or black-mail. Get rid of them and move on.
- If you are single and still healing, save pictures and positive memories; purge negative encounters and unhappy memories.
- Be *for* individuals having success, even your exes.
- Be *against* the mindset of harming, bringing down or seeing others fail.

The Small-Town Vampire Cult has punctured you with a score of wounds. Make a solemn covenant with yourself to never fish in those ponds again and endeavor to take your time, healing slowly.

Where there is a rough or toxic break-up, the loss exceeds just that of the spouse or partner. There is often a loss of friends, church family, or close circle of mutual work colleagues.

In a honorable, clean break-up, friends are retained, support is given and healing occurs. When dealing with a Vampire, a pervasive divisiveness will be present; sides will be forced and friends *stolen*.

Remember, women are smarter than men and the Psychic Femme Vampire has advanced intelligence. She can easily manipulate, seduce and draw average 'everyday guys' away from the Resistant Man, even when he knew them as friends for twenty years before she came on the scene.

She is the victim. She is the empath. She is the introvert. Hers is the narrative to control, especially when you have protected the privacy of your relationship and haven't shared negative comments or occurrences and thus lost the benefit of equal 'air-time'. *She* had privily been badmouthing you to your male friends for months and months before the discard. She was organized. She was ready. You didn't stand a chance.

One-liners and clichés like 'then they weren't your friends to begin with' heal nothing, help nothing, do nothing.

You will see and hear disgusting and troubling things in the immediate months after The Discard. Examples may include:

- Her posing for holiday pictures sitting on the lap of your pastor as if he were Santa Claus and she a nine-year-old. The women in your soon-to-be-former church will be shocked (and tell you as much); the 'elders' will claim neutrality whilst laughing and jesting about the untoward behavior.

- She, the introvert, will suddenly become a social butterfly, posting pictures of herself intentionally 'taking all the boys out' to *your favorite restaurant.*

- You will hear how she hopped on a plane to 'get wise counsel' from the elders (your friends of many, many years) and spent one-on-one time with them... yet she did not so much as have tea with the women in your mutual circle.

- She is suddenly both religious and political (though your interest in those matters bored her to tears during the relationship) and she has ramped up engaging your friends on every post, forum, message board or other setting, where she can 'nestle up to them', and so that you can see the same.

This is all designed, of course, to feed her just a little dessert. The carcass (you) from the main course (your relationship) has been picked clean and resides in the trash. But she is still hungry, wanting some cake, yearning for more psychic energy.

If she lures you into a *Crazy-Making Response* openly, publicly and in front of your mutual friends, it will:

1. Give her more delicious, mouthwatering dessert!

2. Allow her to justify the three hundred and nine false accusations she has already circulated about you.

Here then is the hard truth and recommendation. **Engage in one direct, polite and calm discussion with those who are running round with the woman who has tried to destroy you.** Make your feelings and position known calmly, then walk away. From all of them. Let the death be a full death; loss of narcissist and toxic friends at once, rather than walking around with cancer still cooking in your body.

Should some of your work, church or friend circle see the deep conflict and inappropriateness of their affiliation and endorsement of her, then have an olive branch extended at all times. Be gracious and receive them back into your life, but do not expect it, nor give it place to bother you, neither syphon your positive energy (after a long healing and bereavement process, of course).

And once again, focus on your own policy ensuring that you don't visit this on others, and have helpful lessons to pass onto younger men.

A suggested policy:

1. Govern your life according to principles, this one being vital: *The Principle of the Primacy of Friendship*. This means that whomever had the friend first gets them in the break-up. It is not for you to seduce away her friends (or his, if this is a business relationship or friendship that is terminating) of twenty years. They were hers first; respect that. This is easy, honorable and right.

2. Stick to your own gender. Where intimate friendships are concerned, Boys should be Friends with Boys, and Girls should be Friends with Girls. If your mutual friends are women, and she knew them first, she keeps them. Bottom line.

By honoring and respecting the very real differences between the genders, you will avoid a mountain of troubles, rumors, speculation and self-evident inappropriate appearances in the unfortunate event of a break-up. It is not for you to run around with her girlfriends when your relationship terminates. There are seven billion people on Earth; you have no need to take the three or four that mean most to her.

Engaging mutual friends that are of your own gender is far less inappropriate and will not cause her pain, anguish and dark thoughts of 'what are they saying or doing behind my back?'.

Govern your life according to boundaries and appropriate relationships; honor the primacy of relationships in others; and give no appearance of impropriety or evil.

CHAPTER 27
WHAT TO DO ABOUT IT ALL?

Whereas the former chapters covered 'The Discard' or *when she breaks up with you*, there is another pathway: one where the man has gone so far down the Quiet Man pathway that the Vampire has opted to keep or collect him for periodic energy draining, but has for all intents and purposes entered into infidelity with other 'meals'.

The question that resonates, that pounds throughout any book of this nature, is 'what do you do?'

What do you do! Questing for a helpful magic wand to aid the reader, the actual composition of this work proved resoundingly that all you can do is:

- Forgive
- Extend grace
- Love your neighbor as yourself
- Own your own mistakes. In spite of the harsh nature of some of the content covered herein, all self-actualized adults know that it *takes two to tango*. She's not the Devil, and you, sir, are no angel.
- Never let anyone rob you of your voice – regardless of political correctness, or what is in vogue at the time (or for the generation).

Regarding what to do if you find yourself a drained, befuddled, hurting Quiet Man about to dive into the abyss of a bottle, the recommendation is thus: **Please do everything opposite of what the books tell women to do about men who are narcissists.**

The elite, and by extension their academics, and by extension the heartbroken women-become-Vampires that are seduced by them, teach things contrary to God's word and the nature of reality itself. The lie that the narcissist cannot change means he or she is fated or predetermined to act as they do; they are not responsible for their actions and are thus victims, not villains.

Reject this. We are each one of us responsible for our actions or none of us are, and the elite can't pick and choose who is a victim or villain based upon identity or gender politics. When you realize you may be in love with a 'Covert Narc', find your voice and remind her, as a gentleman, that she is choosing to execute these strategies, that you are aware she is choosing them, that you love her unconditionally, and that you pray she will stop. If convicted by your words, she may again choose to love you (for you love who you love, but every day after is a choice. And the re-investment in the love bank can and often does restore relationships).

She owns it; she is accountable; nothing 'makes her' lie, love-bomb, cheat and screech at you.

And when you say you will pray for her, do so.

The recommendation to just leave her with no contact is from the pit of hell and should be discarded. The 'experts' recommend a no-contact policy for those in, or exiting, a relationship with a narcissist. Ironically, nothing could be more narcissistic than declaring that you are too good, too self-centered, too self-absorbed to abandon, ignore and discard another person, let alone a spouse or serious partner. Communication is the foundation (side by side with Truth) of every relationship, without exception. Even the ones most likely headed for an unfortunate ending.

For the Quiet Man: remove your testicles from the mantle, where she placed them in a jar too long ago, be nice, be firm, and communicate exactly, precisely and with good command your views on what she has done. If she leaves you (likely), then close the door of her hurting you by opening the door that she might change. We should always be at the ready to hear out those who have hurt us, and take authority and power over the situation by offering to help her at any point in the future should she need to reach out.

There is nothing more empowering than doing the right thing. It may bring about a conviction and change in her views, or it may enrage her to expedite a Discard upon you – but regardless of outcome, you will have far more power being kind, communicative and open instead of ditching her.

Moreover, if your desire is for her to leave you alone, the 'honey vs. vinegar' approach may greatly take wind from sails and cause her to lose interest. It is the drama, including the drama of blocking and ignoring someone, that feeds more drama, and more potential for stalking, haranguing, or hassling.

Lastly, love can and does conquer all, and anything short of this truth is a lie designed by those who want more paying clients and patients than healthy, well-adjusted and successful couples.

The real issue with your Covert Narc girlfriend is that her heart was viciously broken, or that she suffered actual and real abuse. She yielded to this horrific stimulus and, giving into temptation (like the other 100% of humanity), let it mold her into a man-hating monster.

She isn't a monster. She isn't a devil. And her vampirism is NOT a death sentence for her. Unfortunately for you, she may not realize this in time to fix or rescue your relationship, but (fortunately) it does mean that she may one day have a very healthy, very successful relationship.

It is a humbling situation. There are many men labeled as narcissists who were abusive maniacs in Relationship A, and wonderful, soft-hearted and sacrificial leaders and lovers in Relationship B.

What changed? Psychotherapy? Medication?

No. They simply didn't love the woman in Relationship A enough to make healthy choices.

The Quiet Man must humble himself and land on the reality that *he is not the one, but not all is lost for her.* We must not pass life sentences on any person in this category. All fall short, and all are redeemable. And love, whether yours or the next guy's, may indeed conquer all.

Men and Women are different. The Man's job, before God, is to exercise an active, daily willingness to die to see that his wife is protected, provided for, honored and adored. Without excuse, and regardless of whether it is returned. The Man's job is to be radically accountable, radically kind, radically warm and radically committed to his partner (and children).

The only sound advice of any merit or weight in the whole of this book rests upon this:

If you would be a Modern-Day Knight – and, what's more, a Man – DO YOUR JOB.

ABOUT THE AUTHOR [2021]

In *Small-Town Psy-Femme-Vampire Cults and the Quiet Man*, author Zane Newitt infuses his distinctive style into an emotional, challenging and refreshing non-fiction work.

Better known for his great saga, *The Arthuriad*, the author is an internationally recognized Arthurian scholar, folklorist and historian who lives in Colorado, USA. In a grueling and personal undertaking, Zane indicates that he "had to get this work out of his basement (the depths of his soul)". Now, having done so, he is most happy to return the world of Arthur, Merlin, Gwenhwyfar and his not-so-veiled advocacy of Welsh Independence, and never revisit the quasi-self-help, relationship, life-issues genre ever again!

PUBLISHER INFORMATION

Rowanvale Books provides publishing services to independent authors, writers and poets all over the globe. We deliver a personal, honest and efficient service that allows authors to see their work published, while remaining in control of the process and retaining their creativity. By making publishing services available to authors in a cost-effective and ethical way, we at Rowanvale Books hope to ensure that the local, national and international community benefits from a steady stream of good quality literature.

For more information about us, our authors or our publications, please get in touch.

www.rowanvalebooks.com
info@rowanvalebooks.com

CPSIA information can be obtained
at www.ICGtesting.com
Printed in the USA
BVHW070819071221
623413BV00007B/317

9 781913 662141